D1008996

ADDICTED TO
sHOPPING
...and Other Issues
Women Have with Money

Karen O'Connor

HARVEST HOUSE PUBLISHERS
EUGENE, OREGON

For Erin,
with love and appreciation.

Keep your lives free
from the love of money
and be content with
what you have,
because God has said,
"Never will I leave you;
never will I forsake you"
(Hebrews 13:5).

Grace and peace be yours in abundance
through the knowledge of God
and of Jesus our Lord
(2 Peter 1:2).

Acknowledgments

I wish to thank the many courageous women who shared with me their experiences, strength, and hope. This book would not have been possible without them. All names and identifying details have been disguised to protect their privacy, unless they gave permission to do otherwise.

I also thank the many professionals who generously opened to me their writings, their research, their expertise, and their observations on the topic of women and debt.

I am grateful to my literary agent, Janet Kobobel Grant, and the staff at Harvest House Publishers for believing in this project and supporting me in completing it.

And finally, I acknowledge and thank my husband, Charles Flowers, for his love and partnership.

Contents

A Word from the Author

A woman's place is in the mall.

Born to shop.

Shop till you drop.

I'd rather be shopping at…

These are just a few of the catchphrases I've seen emblazoned on bumper stickers, coffee mugs, license plate frames, and T-shirts over the past few years. It indicates an increasing trivialization of women and their handling of money. For example, I remember in a hotel gift shop seeing a pair of earrings made to look like American Express cards and another pair resembled two tiny Gucci shopping bags. And recently I attended a women's luncheon and auction to raise money for a charity. One of the items held up for auction was a stuffed toy bear with a little bag on its wrist with the words, "Born to Shop" printed on the front. The following day, while out walking, I noticed in the window of a local boutique a wall hanging for sale with the words "Gone Shopping." Such items give the impression that shopping, spending, and charging are synonymous with being a woman today. I doubt men would purchase such a sign or a mug with similar wording!

Traditionally, women have been the nurturers and purchasers. We hold down jobs by day, and on our lunch hours and weekends we scramble around buying for others: groceries, gifts, kids' clothes, towels and sheets, dog food, garden supplies, bedding, and kitchen items. We generally *see* these needs before the men in our lives do, and so we have taken on the responsibility of providing them. But does that mean we belong in the mall or in the supermarket or in the pet store? Or that once we start shopping we can't stop till we drop? Or that we'd rather be spending than writing a book or waterskiing or growing roses or playing with our children? Whether we work outside the home, own a home-based business, are retired, or are at home rearing our children, we are required to handle money on a daily basis in order to run our households. Money is a powerful resource, and the temptation to abuse it is always there, especially when needs and wants are constantly changing.

Most of us have not been trained well—or at all—when it comes to earning, spending, saving, managing, investing. Couple that with a culture obsessed with money, and we are set up to fall. At the same time, we may overlook what an incredible privilege it is to be the nurturers and spenders, even though it is an increasing challenge to remain balanced and healthy.

Merchants and advertisers feed our desires by making it easy to have everything we want whether or not we can afford it. Maybe we believe that we "owe" it to ourselves to have what we want when we want it—to take advantage of the "unbelievably low prices at the biggest sale of the year" or to "buy now and pay later." In addition, the Internet has ushered in another level of shopping that didn't exist years ago. Women can now shop till they drop sitting at home in front of their own computers.

And the women who have managed to stay out of the mall and away from the Internet? Where are they? Many are terrified to shop or spend because they're afraid they'll use up what money they do have—and then what? Such women claim they are as unhealthy around money as the biggest spender or gambler or charge-card abuser. Such nonspenders don't have peace. Money rules. They too think about it, fear it, dream about it, talk about it, and obsess over it.

Between these two groups are millions of other women who do not spend, shop, charge, or gamble, but they are caught up in money madness because they support, enable, and cover up for the people they love who are financially messed up. Money runs their lives through husbands, boyfriends, parents, and children. Even if right now you're saying you don't fit any of these cubbyholes, consider the fact that you're reading this book. Maybe, as I did, you are beginning to feel the craziness gradually. You can't quite put your finger on it, but you feel weird about money. It makes you edgy or fearful or anxious. You want to run away from it. You wish it would go away or that someone would handle it for you. Or at the very least, you may wish you had more of it or had more control over what you do have.

Related to these categories is something I call *self-debt*—a state I know very well. It's a state of being that forms the basis of all other behaviors around money, a state that keeps the craziness going. A self-debtor is a woman who compulsively gives away her money, her strength, her energy, her ideas, sometimes her very life—to her mate, children, parents, and friends. She needs their love, their approval, their acceptance…and she will do whatever it takes to get it. To some degree, most women have challenges with self-debt—partly because we are the caretakers and nurturers. We want things to be well with those we love, and if we can help them, then of course we want to.

- When a woman puts other people's needs before her own, she is a self-debtor.

- When a woman consistently earns less than she knows she is worth, she is a self-debtor.

- When a woman stops earning or saving money the minute she gets involved in a relationship with a man, she is a self-debtor.

- When a woman spends money on everyone but herself, she is a self-debtor.

- When a woman buys things she neither wants nor needs, she is a self-debtor.

☀ When time and again she overspends on food, clothing, trinkets, gifts, or vacations to alter her mood, she is a self-debtor.

This book is a direct result of my own experiences with money and relationships. It also includes the experiences and concerns of women I've spoken with directly and the many who have attended workshops where I have spoken on this topic.

In this book you will meet some of these women—overspenders, shopaholics, credit-card abusers, gamblers, debt enablers, under-earners, self-debtors, and perpetual paupers. I do not focus on how to earn more and spend less, though you may discover how to do that as you read about the experiences of these women. Such matters are well-covered in other books, and I've listed some of them in the back under Supplementary Resources.

Instead, my focus is on *the abuse and misuse of money* as it affects us emotionally and spiritually. My purpose is to support you in recognizing where your weaknesses are with money, understanding their origins, and gaining tools for change and growth. To help you accomplish this, I have divided the book into four parts.

In Part 1, we'll discuss the shame and anxiety many of us feel when it comes to money and how and why we got this way. In Part 2, we'll meet women—decent, loving, caring people—who have problems with money. As you read their stories, I hope you will draw on their experiences and strength and use them to chart your own path.

Part 3 is about putting a stop to the madness by facing the truth about ourselves, about others, about God. And Part 4 reveals the joy of living that is available once we discover the truth for ourselves.

Change and growth are not really about money after all. They're about achieving spiritual, emotional, mental, and physical well-being. You may find, too, that your most important creditor is *you,* and that as you become well in your relationship with money, God will lead and direct you to what's next: "I guide you in the way of wisdom and lead you along straight paths" (Proverbs 4:11).

The pressing need today is not for more women of independent means or for more intelligent, creative, or assertive women. No, the need is for women of spiritual substance, women willing to make the inward journey to the deep treasures of the spirit.

By bringing into balance your *inner account,* you will be in a better position to attract the money, the job, and the relationships that will support you in being the person you want to be and having all the good God has for you—the good you desire and truly deserve. I consider it a privilege to walk the path with you.

—Karen O'Connor

Part 1

Money
Madness

1
Secret Shame

A tall, striking woman appeared in the doorway behind me at a weekly support meeting. She paused for a moment, then found a place at the table directly across from me. I had not seen her before, so I assumed she was new.

"I'm Audrey," she said in a loud whisper. The man next to her shook her hand and said, "Welcome."

I was drawn to Audrey from the moment I saw her. So were the men in the room! I guessed her to be about my age at the time—fiftyish. She had style and grace, like a beautiful willow. I even admired the way she eased herself into the straight-backed chair. Her movements were as fluid as a summer breeze.

Her straight chestnut-colored hair, drawn back, exposed a beautiful face. Her full lips glistened with just the right shade of lipstick, and her cheeks were highlighted with a brush of red, the perfect touch beneath large, deep-brown eyes.

The thin gold chain around her neck, an array of slender bracelets on her left arm, and enormous hoop earrings set off the simple cream-colored silk blouse she wore. *It all works*, I thought to myself. *Here's a lady who knows how to put herself together.*

My mind wandered for a moment. *A model. I bet she's a model for Nordstrom or Saks Fifth Avenue*, I told myself. *Then what's she doing here? At a meeting for people with money problems? She looks like she could buy and sell whatever she wanted.*

I hoped she'd tell her story.

As the hour went on and various people shared their experiences and feelings, I noticed Audrey's eyes mist on several occasions. She pulled out a handkerchief, dabbed the corners of her eyes, shifted nervously in her chair, and then folded and unfolded her hands on the table in front of her. The bright-red polish on her impeccably manicured nails created a pleasing contrast to her fair skin.

Suddenly she was speaking. I couldn't wait to hear what she had to say. "I'm Audrey." She introduced herself, blinking back tears. "I'm in trouble with money. I don't know a thing about how to manage it. I feel like a child," she said softly, "yet I'm 52 years old. I'm divorced. I have three grown children. I was married to a prominent corporate attorney in Great Neck, Long Island—that's in New York," she added, perhaps assuming Californians might not know the location.

"And I'm $30,000 in debt." She lowered her head as a young girl might after making a true confession. "I don't know how it happened. Actually, I never had enough money after the divorce. I was always behind. It was easy to use my credit cards," she added. "The banks make them so appealing." A faint smile crossed her lips.

"My husband and I had been married for 25 years. We were comfortable, or so I thought. We had everything—the cars, the club, the clothes, a home in the city and a summer place in Montauk.

"Then he met someone playing golf, and that was the beginning of the end. It was as if he had been waiting for an excuse to leave me."

Suddenly Audrey broke down. She sobbed softly at first, and then everyone in the room probably heard her. I choked back my own tears. This was *my* story, almost word for word. It was about a different town and a different husband, but the details were nearly the same.

She had been raised in a family much like my own. A solid Midwestern family with solid values. We went to church. We took family vacations. We entertained family and friends. We had a good, comfortable life. We even spent part of one summer on Montauk Point.

Like Audrey, I attended a small Christian college for women, graduated, married a law student, struggled through the bar exam with him, had three babies in five years, and woke up 20 years later realizing my husband was having an affair. Soon after, we were divorced and I was alone with my children, frightened and overwhelmed with broken relationships, a devastated self-image, and no sense of how to handle, spend, invest, or deal with money. I was a child in a 41-year-old body.

I wanted to put my arms around Audrey, give her a hug, and let her know we're all in this together. But that would come later. For now I knew she needed to cry, to let out the grief and shame—the terrible secret shame we feel as women when we're finally willing to admit that we are alone, scared, and penniless…that we fear ending up on the street or stuck in a spare room in someone else's home. The shame of driving a 12-year-old car when all our adult lives we've had a new car every two years. The pain of watching friends' marriages weather the storms of affairs and graduate school and sick kids and aging parents, knowing ours didn't make it. Believing that somehow we aren't enough—not pretty enough, thin enough, sexy enough, patient enough. Deep in our guts we honestly believe we're defective in some way that can never be fixed.

Audrey's soft voice startled me out of my thoughts. "I have seven charge cards," she said. "It's the only way I've been able to survive. I've never had a real career. I considered modeling when I was younger, but then I married, and the children came, and—well you know the story," she said, looking around the room.

"I have almost nothing to show for the divorce. I netted about $100,000, but I went through that in three years. I tried to make wise decisions. I talked to people and invested in some land. But it's gone. Every penny is gone.

"I'm working at Nordstrom now. I moved here last year after my last son was married. I decided it was time for a change…time to think of myself, though I'm not very good at that.

"I worked at Macy's when I was in high school, so selling women's clothing seemed like something I could do. I made $25,000 last year, and I have $5,000 more than that in debt! A friend of mine figured out that at 20 percent annually, I owe $500 a month in interest alone. That's exactly my share of the rent where I'm living."

Debt Trap

Audrey is not the only woman (or man) trapped by debt. According to a 2003 report from Debtscape, a non-profit debt counseling organization, the average family carries a balance of $4000 from month-to-month on several credit cards. The typical minimum monthly payment is 90 percent interest and 10 percent principal.

"If you didn't have your credit-card payment of $218 a month, and you instead invested that money in a 12 percent savings plan, in 25 years you could retire with $1,354,930 in the bank. So your credit-card payments not only will cost you thousands in interest, but also prohibit many Americans from adequately saving for their retirement."

For people with such high debt compared to their income and assets, bankruptcy often seems to be the only option. And many take that route. But those in 12-step recovery groups, such as Debtors Anonymous, Gamblers Anonymous (based on the model of Alcoholics Anonymous), and other solvency programs have discovered that "debting" is an emotional disease much like alcoholism, overeating, and drug abuse. It is a disease that, without help, never gets better. In fact, it gets worse over time. Bankruptcy simply delays the inevitable *unless* a person takes steps to recover.

Bankruptcy doesn't work because being in debt is not really a *money* issue. It is an issue of self-worth and our feelings of not being enough. Women in debt try to fill the emptiness inside by spending money on themselves or others.

Audrey and I—and every other woman I know who is in debt—struggle with the same basic issue—a poor self-image. The emotional hole in each one of us is so big you could drive a truck through it. New clothes, a new car, or a new relationship won't fill it. Spurts of generous giving to others won't fill it either.

When these things don't work, many of us go to the other extreme. We become misers, hoarding our money, denying ourselves even basic clothing, nourishing food, adequate housing. And when that doesn't work either, some women in debt consider suicide. Rhonda said, "One year I was so despondent over my credit-card bills that I told myself if I couldn't get a handle on them before the end of the year, I'd just end it. Then I found Debtors Anonymous, and through the program I learned to surrender to a power greater than myself—God—and that was the turning point for me."

The steps to change are not set in stone. You may wish to map out your own plan based on what you read here. But the point is *women who surrender their will to God, then plan and take action, do get well.* It's that simple—and that challenging.

Depending on when and where you were raised, you have absorbed "lessons" about money. Women currently in their 20s and 30s have been brought up in a culture that proclaims, "You can have it if you want it" and "You deserve it." This creates a me-centered viewpoint. It is difficult for such a woman to delay gratification. A new SUV or sportscar she can pay for "on time" is more attractive than a modest used car she can afford. The $100 pair of designer jeans is a must-have regardless of the fact that it might take 20 percent of the spender's gross weekly income.

If you are over 40, you too, have learned your lessons well. The very traits that may have contributed to your trouble with money in the first place—self-denial and loyalty in the extreme plus unrealistic submission and service—are often those admired as feminine and nurturing. But they can also be confused with true "other-centeredness," which is the biblical principle that Jesus modeled perfectly. He cared for others, but he never interfered with their ability to make decisions for themselves. He offered friendship and hospitality and loving support, but he didn't force them to follow him. If he was turned down, he moved on. He did not give in order to get or take care of in order to feel better about himself.

This is an important distinction to make. When we support and stand *with* another person, we are energized and they are empowered to make wise choices. But if we push, pull, and prod, the strain wears down both people, and we are more likely then to spend, gamble, charge, or hoard in a desperate attempt to give ourselves something—anything—to avoid reality.

Like Audrey, you did not suddenly become crazy around money. Neither did I. The problem started years ago when we were growing up. How we got that way and what we can do about it is the subject of this book. But first I want to introduce another woman, someone quite different from Audrey and me—and yet a woman exactly the same in many ways.

The Clean Scene: Kathleen's Story

"I realize now I've always had a problem with money," said the petite brunette in her mid-thirties. "I guess you could call it my last secret. I'd rather talk about anything else—sex, my job, religion, my boyfriend, you name it. Anything but money. The whole subject of debt, credit cards, spending plans, and budgeting terrifies me. I've never had enough money, and if I did I wouldn't know what to do with it anyway."

Kathleen's eyes filled up as she shared her story. "Last week it really hit me. I was standing on a ladder washing my apartment windows. All of a sudden I realized what I was doing. This was my fourth apartment in three years, and I'd scrubbed every one of them. I have a cleaning fetish," she added, laughing nervously. "It probably sounds ridiculous, but it's true.

"I believe it started the summer I turned ten. Until that year, my family lived on a small two-acre chicken farm in the Midwest. Then we lost everything. I'm still not sure how or why. It's one of those family secrets that no one talks about. Anyway, my dad was so devastated when the farm went under that he couldn't work for months. We moved to a small rented house in town. Then a friend of his offered him a part-time job washing windows and cleaning offices at night and on weekends. He continued that job till I was out of high school."

Kathleen pushed up the sleeves of her denim shirt, ran a hand through her short hair, and sighed deeply. "That particular summer I remember my father telling me I was old enough to help him wash windows. He said he could use a helper but didn't have enough money to hire someone. He thought I'd be a great window washer. I felt special standing beside him—he on one ladder and I on another. He even took me to the store with him to buy the supplies.

"After that, whenever my dad had more work than he could do by himself, I got to help. In fact, those are the only times I remember spending any time with him." Kathleen laughed, sniffed back the tears, and nervously wiped her nose with the back of her hand.

"He didn't believe in socializing," she continued. "'Waste of time,' he used to say. And he had a rule about money after we lost the farm. I'll never forget it. Money is for 'necessaries,' he said. And dancing lessons or pretty clothes or eating out definitely were not on that list.

"One of his most often-repeated statements was, 'We don't have money for that.' Yet there had been plenty of money for paint and lumber and chicken feed when we lived on the farm and for his cleaning supplies and his truck in town—important things that would last, he said. So my mother and I shopped garage sales and thrift stores for clothes. In my whole childhood I don't think I ever had an article of clothing that cost more than a dollar or two, and never ever something new."

Kathleen doodled on a piece of paper as she talked. "Cleaning, fixing things up—it's all I know. That's hard to face. As I stood on the ladder washing the windows, it was like I was ten years old all over again. I wondered if my dad would approve. He's been dead for five years, but I've gone right on washing windows, wanting him to be proud of me."

Her voice escalated for a moment, then mellowed. "I even got a thrill out of buying a new bucket and new blades and a can of paint. I raced through the hardware store like most women run through Macy's or Mervyn's. I put $200 worth of stuff on my Visa card in less than an hour. "Necessaries," she said with a laugh. "All of it for an *apartment* that I *rent*. Who knows how long I'll live there? And yet I went into debt again so I could *clean*. And I have never ever spent $200 on myself at one time. Never!"

Silence settled over the room like a blanket. Women around the table were beginning to see and hear themselves in Kathleen's story.

"Even my clothes are the same. These jeans are eight years old. Got 'em at a garage sale. Fifty cents! The same with shoes and shirts. I own two dresses. I got both of them at a thrift shop. I'm 34 years old, but I'm still living like that 10-year-old kid, terrified to spend money on myself, yet up to my ears in debt for 'necessaries' like my truck. Can you believe that? I drive a truck, just like my dad did."

Audrey and Kathleen, like millions of other women, grew up in families where money was used to manipulate and control, to alter moods, to rescue, to reinforce certain kinds of behavior. As adults, such women find themselves using money in the same destructive way—building debts by indulging in things they neither need nor really want. Nor can they afford them.

Or they find themselves in the opposite camp, terrified to spend money for fear of unleashing its power over them. Still others go into debt by rescuing someone else. They buy into every hard-luck story they hear, financing a car for a teenage son, taking out a second mortgage on a home to help a boyfriend pay off his consumer debts, allowing a divorced friend to move in rent-free.

Before we can fully appreciate and understand the underpinnings of this compulsive behavior, however, I think it would be helpful to look at several ways we can define debt.

What Is Debt?

Debt, pure and simple, is money or service owed to a creditor—a person or an institution. In the world of finance, there are two kinds of debt: *secured* and *unsecured*. To secure something is to make it safe. A secured loan is kept safe for the lender by means of *collateral*—an item of equal or greater value, which the lender holds during the repayment period. The pink slip on your car, for example, is collateral for your automobile loan. If you can't keep up your payments, the lender repossesses your car. You lose your car (and your credit rating), but you don't owe any more money. The lender does not lose money either because he now has your car—a good example of Proverbs 22:7: "The borrower is servant to the lender."

Any time you pledge a piece of property—a computer, a life insurance policy, jewelry, real estate, stock certificate—as collateral for a sum of money you borrow, you have entered into a secured loan—not secured for you, but for the lender. And you risk losing that security. Technically you could say that a secured loan is not really a debt since the item or property of equal value keeps you accountable for repayment. But for women with compulsive behavior around money, even a secured loan can be a powerful and destructive tool.

On the surface, it may seem perfectly in order to purchase a car or a piece of office equipment on an installment plan. However, such a loan also feeds into the cycle of debt many women are trying to break. And in the event they cannot keep up the payments, the car or equipment is repossessed, fueling the self-hatred and helplessness that provoked going into debt in the first place. In my experience, a woman is better off paying cash or doing without until she has embarked on a disciplined program of recovery.

Unsecured loans are another matter. Groceries, clothing, cosmetics, restaurant dining, gas for your car, theater tickets, and other items you charge on your MasterCard, Visa, American Express, or Diners Club accounts are not tied to collateral. Neither are spontaneous loans ($50 till payday, $10 for a pizza) made between family and friends.

Unsecured debt is where we get into the most trouble. We have bought the lie "buy now; pay later." And we do *pay* in more ways than one, which brings up the *emotional* side of debt, where we spend or borrow or loan money without regard for our well-being.

This behavior is usually compulsive, meaning we don't think about it rationally or consciously. We act this way to avoid unpleasant feelings of pain, fear, and grief. We can't stop no matter how hard we try, no matter how much we know. Spending, in whatever form, takes the place of feeling the authentic emotion.

Self-Debt

Compulsive spending, when driven by the unconscious, leads to a more subtle form of debt—something called *self-debt*. Self-debt is also money or services owed to a creditor. The creditor, however, is *you.*

Most debt, secured or unsecured, is self-debt. When we use goods and services without paying for them immediately, we not only take from the creditor, but we also take from ourselves. Self-worth, integrity, and personal responsibility fall as we depend on others to do for us what we can and should do for ourselves—pay as we go.

The reverse is also true. When we take from ourselves to do for others what they can and should do for themselves, we go into self-debt. When we rescue or help boyfriends, husbands, and adult children capable of earning, we rob them of the opportunity to work through their own problems, to discover their own resources. And in the process, we steal from ourselves—money, time, energy, goods, or services that are necessary to our own survival and well-being.

Giving to Get

Does that mean we never give a gift, help a friend in desperate straits, or lend a hand to a struggling adult child? Of course not. It is one thing to offer honest assistance within the limits of time and available resources. It is quite another matter, however, to give in order to get, which is often the case with women in debt. Our motives are generally more intense than those of women who merely wish to buy a new car or provide a night or two of shelter for a friend in need.

Our motives often go back to childhood. We spend, borrow, or loan money in order to feel better about ourselves, to gain the attention, affection, and approval that we missed out on while growing up. We help capable adult friends with mortgage and car payments. We turn over our gas cards to teenage children. We charge a new suit on our Visa card for our boyfriend or mate so he can interview for a job. We buy our parents hundred-dollar gifts when our budget or spending plan clearly prohibits such extravagance.

On the outside our motives may appear generous, even loving. On the inside, however, we know differently. Giving to, taking care of, and providing for others raises our self-image and alters our mood. We are actually giving in order to get—to get that good feeling, to get the approval and affection of someone else, to get out of an unpleasant mood.

I remember two months in a row when my husband and I received financial aid from the Deacon's Fund at our church in order to pay our rent. I was humiliated. I had always prided myself on *giving* to the fund for the needy. I never anticipated being a recipient. That experience showed me how resistant I was to being vulnerable. I was much more comfortable and in control as the giver.

This experience also showed me an important difference between a woman who gives "no strings attached" and the type of woman who gives in order to get something for herself. Those who give because they cannot risk being vulnerable are *compelled* to give. Compulsive giving creates a sense of power and authority. Such women *must* give. Some of them believe, as I did, that it is the *right* thing to do. Others don't even think about it to that extent. They do it quite simply because, at some level, they *have* to. They charge, loan, spend, borrow, give, take, hoard, lose, or gamble time and again. And then they wonder where all their money went, why there never seems to be enough, why *they* seemingly are never enough.

Debt—no matter how you define it or speak about it or use it—is real. Being in debt is a *serious* condition. It should never be taken lightly. It has the potential to destroy everyone and everything important to you— family, jobs, friends, your marriage, even your health, as millions of women in debt can attest to.

Such women, by their own admission, use debt to manipulate their own and other people's lives, to cover up their feelings, to punish or reward themselves, to help or hold hostage family and friends. To a woman who feels unhealthy around money, any reason will do. You may be one of them. If you are, you may recognize in yourself some or all of the following characteristics that seem to be present in the lives of such women.

1. *Typically, you grew up in an emotionally distant home.*

   You did not see honest displays of anger, joy, sadness, love, or grief. Perhaps you were quieted down when you became excited, or you were told to "cool it," or to consider others, or not to make noise or show your temper. You may have been rewarded in some way for being the even-tempered one or the "dependable" child.

Beyond that, your perceptions of your own feelings may have been ignored or denied. "Don't tell me you're sad. There's nothing to be sad about." "If you complain one more time I'll give you something to be upset about—something you'll never forget."

If you told your mother that your brother hurt your feelings, she may have told you to "be a big girl" or not to "make a mountain out of a molehill." Parents or grandparents have used some other clichés that, in summary, told you to stuff your feelings, that your feelings didn't count.

2. *You manipulate other people regarding money issues.*

   You may have learned as a child to manipulate your parents or others through spending. A new dress, an ice cream cone, or the latest game satisfied you for the moment. Over time you saw how easy it was to get the attention you needed. Display strong feelings, and someone would spend money on you. It became a way of life.

3. *You spend money in order to change your feelings.*

   You may be threatened by feelings of rage, jealousy, or anger. You "handle" them by treating yourself to something new—a quick trip through Target, a few necessities at Costco, a sweater on sale at Wal-Mart, or a must-have at Nordstrom. Within an hour or so you feel better, lighter, happier. Even if you don't have the cash to pay for these items, it's no problem. You can charge them. No need to worry today over what doesn't have to be paid for till next month.

4. *You accept the message that you are not important enough to spend money on.*

   Perhaps you discovered early that there wasn't enough money for you. Money was for important things such as cars and furniture and rent…or other members of your household. Someone in your family may have consistently reminded you that "money doesn't grow on trees," as if you thought it did. If you were a younger child in your family, you may have grown accustomed to wearing hand-me-down clothes, and if you longed for something brand-new just for you, you were led to feel guilty.

As an adult you cannot bring yourself to buy even the necessities. You make that pair of shoes work yet another season. You mend the blouse and patch the jeans. "They're good enough," you tell yourself. "Money doesn't grow on trees."

5. *You equate spending with emotional fulfillment.*

Every spring and fall you're the first one in line for the sales at the local department stores. You're not sure why, but you're always there. You remember your mother taking you shopping for school clothes and summer shorts and bathing suits. They were special times for you.

Shopping and lunch at a nice restaurant with your mother twice a year set the pattern in motion. You remember her smiling and admiring you in your new things. You returned home filled up inside and feeling pretty on the outside. Today you're looking for that same emotional fulfillment, even if you have to spend money to get it.

6. *You associate spending with excitement.*

Perhaps your father traveled as a salesman. He never knew where his next check was coming from. The entire family lived on the edge. When sales were up, there were new clothes, ice cream for dessert, and maybe a summer vacation. When sales were down, your parents sold the car or some of the furniture. You never knew what to expect, but one thing for sure—it was never dull at your house. Today you keep yourself broke, living from paycheck to paycheck, in order to keep the drama going, to feel alive.

7. *You fear the power of money so you avoid it by under-earning.*

   For many women, money appears to have a life of its own. If you allow yourself to have a penny more than you absolutely need, you fear losing control. To ensure your safety, you take dead-end, no-stress jobs that keep you safe…and stuck. You wouldn't dream of owning a comfortable car, or wearing a silk blouse, or taking an art class, or enrolling in a graduate program, or signing up for a cruise. Those things are for people with money, people with power, people who like to flaunt their prosperity. Or so you've been told. Women who consistently and deliberately under-earn are terrified to give themselves permission to be creative, exciting, attractive, and intellectually stimulating. Nice girls should be seen and not heard.

8. *You feel worthy only when you spend money on others.*

   If you grew up in a home where your mother was a full-time caregiver, then your sense of worth may be directly connected to how much you do for others and how little you do for yourself. You may be the kind of woman who would rather go into debt than cut down on gift-giving. You are the one to buy a bag of groceries for the needy family, write a check for a friend's car payment, or provide music lessons and birthday parties for your children or grandchildren, even if it means you go without needed clothing or necessary dental care. Spending money on other people makes you feel good about yourself. You *have* to do it.

9. *You feel helpless and childlike around money issues.*

   Just thinking about money brings on a migraine. You've never had a head for figures. You hate numbers and columns and checkbooks. You can't be bothered with all this financial planning business.

   Anyway, you're sure things will work out. They always do. They'll never get totally out of control. And if they do, well, there's bound to be someone to take care of you. You're a child at heart, carefree and innocent. You believe it's the way God made you. And you aim to stay that way, even if it costs you everything.

10. *You live in a state of terminal vagueness.*

Yes, you have a savings account, you think. You do keep track of your checks, but you round off the balance to make it easy. If you forget your check ledger, you jot down the number and amount on a napkin and stuff it in your purse. You can enter it later. Or you stop at an ATM machine and pull out some cash, not clear whether or not you have enough. You have some notion about your financial picture, but it's fuzzy. You can't quite bring it into focus. You're terminally vague.

11. *You're addicted to money, whether you spend or hoard.*

You don't touch alcohol. You never overeat. But your substance of choice is money. You either spend it as fast as you get it or you stash it away to the point of insanity, depriving yourself of even basic human needs. Everything in your life revolves around how much money is involved.

If a friend invites you to a movie and lunch, your first thought is, "How much is it going to cost me?" If you see an ad for a weekend camping trip to the desert, you look at the cost first, your need for a break, second. If someone gives you a gift of money for your birthday or other occasion, you put it into the bank immediately. You never even consider spending it as it was intended—on a gift for yourself.

12. *You have little sense of your worth as a person.*

You are an expert on what other people need and want and deserve, but you have no idea what is good for you. You never stop long enough to find out. This lack of insight keeps you from making wise and healthy choices for your own well-being. But you haven't known that because you don't know your worth as a person, as a woman, as a child of God.

Instead of expressing your feelings and allowing them to help you make important decisions, you stand on the sidelines wringing your hands. So out of touch are you with your own needs and wishes that you continually fret over money and puzzle over such basic decisions as what to buy, what to wear, what to eat, where to go, even what to think.

In the following pages, women like you share their stories about their relationships with money—stories that may help you see and understand more clearly your particular patterns. Many of the stories have happy endings…or beginnings, depending on your point of view. These women are in recovery programs where they are dealing with the emotional issues that have for too long fueled their unhealthy relationship with money. And most have discovered that relating to God, right now in the moment, is the *first* step toward true change.

My hope is that their courage and their testimonies will cause you to take action in your own life. Freedom, as you will see and experience, is available to any woman who claims it. The first and most important step is being willing to recognize your need to change and make it a priority.

2
Crazy Around Money

Linda, a widow aged 57, says she's been nuts around money for as long as she can remember. She's never known any other way of living. Her parents borrowed money for everything from school tuition to a tractor for the family farm. She grew up borrowing, and she's continued the pattern—a pattern she's now trying to break.

Esther said her home while growing up was one of pride and discipline. "We're the Parsons," her father repeated proudly throughout her childhood. "We don't take anything from anybody. If we can't pay for it, we can't have it." Esther remembers longing for a bicycle—even a used one. But in a family of seven children, there wasn't enough money for such things. And there was no discussing the fact that she could have earned the money for the bike. It was understood that only her brothers could work.

"I vowed then that one day I'd have a bicycle," she said. "I didn't care what it would take. And later, when I was on my own, I bought that bicycle the only way I knew how—on credit. Ironically, someone stole it just two months later, and that was the end of that." Esther looked heavenward. "Except for the payments," she said. "For the next year I continued paying for the bike I would never ride again."

My own ride with debt began the summer I married my first husband. We were living in a furnished one-bedroom apartment in Southern

California and had everything we needed for the time being except a television set.

We wanted one, and we saw no reason to wait. We even rationalized that if we had this entertainment center at home we'd spend less money on movies and other outside amusements.

We had enough cash from wedding gifts to pay outright, but we decided, instead, to buy it "on time," to build a credit history. I remember the thrill of purchasing this first piece of furniture together. We walked into the store, chose the set we wanted, and took it home. We still had our savings intact, and we had only a small monthly payment over the next year. It was so simple—so simple, in fact, that for the next 20 years of our marriage we were never again out of debt.

How and Why

How and why we get crazy around money is a complex issue. I doubt that any one of us chooses—at least consciously—to abuse money. It's not a decision we make, such as going to graduate school or starting a family or joining a gym. That's why it's so insidious and so baffling to most of us.

However, when we stop and look around us today, we can see the signs everywhere. Our culture demands that we look a certain way, own certain things, and behave in certain ways. Ads tell us we aren't good enough just the way we are. The reality TV show "Swan," for example, focused on plastic surgery, straight white teeth, slim hips, big breasts, and great hair! And women lined up to audition for it.

Trends rule. Today there is a trend toward simpler living. There is even a magazine called *Real Simple*. And there are books that tell us how to downsize, eliminate clutter, organize our possessions. But even "simpler" living costs money. We rush out to pick up the products that promise simplicity. Often they cost more than the products we've been using for years. We are bombarded with sales pitches whether overtly or covertly through billboards, catalogs, e-mail, websites, sitcoms, and television shopping channels.

We must begin paying attention to *how* we get into debt so we can gain some understanding of *why*. It usually starts with the little things.

Borrowing from Family and Friends

"I never carry cash," says 31-year-old Rita. "I know if I have it, I'll spend it. But I guess that doesn't make sense because I end up borrowing from friends and then spending their money for coffee and lunch or a movie. I've lost a lot of friends that way. I always plan to pay them back, and sometimes I do. But I never seem to get caught up. I always owe somebody something, and half the time I don't remember how much or who I owe it to."

Bouncing Checks

Leslie is in the habit of bouncing checks. She says she's not a thief. She's just an underpaid, overworked county social worker who rewards herself at the end of a hard case with something pretty, something nice, something clearly not in her budget. "I keep telling myself I'm going to wait till I know I have enough in the bank, but then I see a dress, or a piece of jewelry, or a book and I just have to have it. For the last few years I feel like I've spent most of my free time dodging calls from the bank and closing and starting new accounts."

Kiting Checks

Marta, on the other hand, writes checks for more than she has in her account—especially the week before payday. She cashes a check at the supermarket on Friday night and hopes it won't clear before she can deposit her paycheck the following Monday. *Kiting* is the name of this game—one many women play from time to time and get away with. Today, most stores are able to verify funds before accepting a check, but some still do not have the equipment for this. Check kiters create a list of places that accept checks without bank verification and then jump from one to another to keep their habit going.

Buying Things We Don't Need or Want

Renee said her debts involve things she doesn't need or want. "I have a Cuisinart food processor I never use because I hate to cook. I have a gold Cross pen and pencil set that I've never taken out of the box. And I even have a gorgeous piece of Samsonite luggage, yet I don't travel. I can't tell you what all this means. I vaguely remember thinking that if I have the right equipment, maybe I'll feel more like cooking or writing letters or taking a trip. It's nuts," she said with a wave of her hand.

"Actually, I see how I'm like my mother in this. She always had a lot of stuff around the house she never used. I remember a sewing machine that sat in the corner of our dining room for years. She didn't sew, and I never once saw it open. When I asked her if she was going to start making clothes for my sister and me, she said, 'I just might do that one day. I just might do that.' And that was the last time we ever talked about it.

"Another time my brother and I snooped in her closet to see what she got us for Christmas, and I saw this gorgeous red wool coat with a tag on it and a beautiful hat with fur trim. I had never seen her wear either one. I couldn't ask her about them because then she'd know we'd gone into her closet. But I wondered about that coat and hat for a long time afterward. Then the thoughts faded away until I began talking to my therapist about my childhood." Renee took a deep breath and looked out the window.

"Maybe someday I'll have the courage to ask my mother about it. But then I'd have to admit that I looked into her closet," she said with a childlike giggle. "I wonder if she'd be mad at me after all these years."

Shopping to Feel Better

Annette says playfully that she was born to shop. "Something special happens in a mall," she says. "It's magic. The colors and fabrics, the sounds, and the window displays. I've always been hooked on clothes, especially since I did some modeling as a teenager. My mother backed me on this and my dad paid. But I'm 34 now, and he's not picking up the bills anymore. I spent nearly $8,000 on clothes this year, and I only make $35,000.

Buying What We Cannot Afford

"I had worked for six years straight without a vacation," said Dana, with a note of self-pity in her voice. "As far as I was concerned I deserved that cruise," she said, talking about a recent ten-day trip to the Bahamas. "I'll probably be paying for it for the next five years, but it was worth it."

Lucy, who lives in Oregon, said she bought a new, larger car when her parents, sister, and brother-in-law made plans to visit her one year for the Christmas holidays. "I knew I couldn't get everyone into my little VW, so I bought a new four-door Honda. All I was doing was spending money—trying to make a nest for myself. I bought a set of china for six, placemats, napkins, the whole deal. And I spent $100 on tree ornaments. I wanted desperately for my family to see that I was doing well."

Lucy said she never told them that she had to take out a huge loan to cover all these expenditures. "It's ridiculous when I look back now," she said. "They could have rented a car for the few days they were here, and we could have used the plastic dishes I had on hand. I haven't used the china or the napkins since their visit four years ago. And a small tree with some colored lights and balls would have been sufficient. I'm still paying for that spending spree—in more ways than one."

Putting Other People's Financial Needs First

Betty, a 65-year-old widow, is, by her own admission, a perfect example of putting others first to her own detriment. When her husband died, he left her a house that was paid for and a $500,000 life-insurance policy. "That was five years ago," she said wistfully, "and most of my assets are gone—except the house. And I'll lose that if I don't get a handle on this spending. As you can see," she said, pointing to her clothes, "I'm not exactly ready for the Saks runway. I haven't bought myself a new piece of clothing in years. Actually, I don't need anything.

"My kids are my downfall. They're all struggling with mortgage payments and orthodontia for my grandkids and car repairs—and, well, you know what it's like. We've all been through it. I can't stand watching them suffer through these lean years. I bought my one son a car, and I gave my daughter and her husband the down payment on a condo and on and on it goes. I'm an absolute sucker when it comes to my kids. I figure I can do without, but they shouldn't have to. Of course they don't have a clue that I've gone through this much money so fast. My son would kill me if he knew. That's why I've got to get some help before it's too late."

Gambling to Relieve Stress

Joan likes to play a game of cards once in a while—for money—or bet on a race at the race track or buy a lottery ticket. At least that's the way it started. Now she says all she can think about is the next bet. "There's something about picking those numbers, or choosing a horse, or going for the winning hand. I can't explain it," she said. "It makes me feel good, alive, excited again." But Joan doesn't go to the track or the card room or the lottery window occasionally or just for fun anymore. Betting and gambling have become a way of life with her. She needs help.

Beliefs and Behaviors

We want to change our out-of-control behavior. The danger in wanting to change, however, is being impatient and naive about the process. It's important to recognize that we didn't get this way overnight, and we won't change overnight. The highway to health—like any highway—has restaurants and markets, shopping malls and car dealerships. We cannot stop using money in the same way a recovering alcoholic can stop drinking or an addict can stop using drugs. We must spend money, even as we stop abusing it.

We must learn to view money in a new way—as a means of exchange—not as a magic wand! A good first step is observing our habits and practices with money. But our search can't stop there. What we're really after is *a system of beliefs that keeps the unwanted behavior in place.*

Kathy Miller, prosperity coach, founder of "A Good Steward," and youth advisor with her husband at the church they attend, knows what makes people tick when it comes to money. She can spot the beliefs that "run" people, often before they notice them.

Over the past ten years Kathy has been "in board rooms and living rooms, in recording studios and artists' studios, in makeshift home offices and at kitchen tables helping individuals overcome their financial hurdles so they can move on to living life fully, expressing their passion, and sharing their gifts."[1]

She teaches her clients how to cut through financial clutter so they can create powerful results, such as having a budget that works, a savings plan, money for tithing, and funds for vacations and emergencies. There is a smile in her voice as she talks about the courage and commitment it takes to accept the challenge of changing long-standing beliefs and chaotic behavior regarding money and, in her words, "Grow for it!"

What are some of the beliefs that keep women stuck in self-defeating patterns with money? She mentions a few...

We Believe Our Daydreams

Women often make important decisions based on what they learned growing up, what they *perceive* to be true, and what they dream about and wish for. Then they have to live with those choices forever—to their detriment! For example, a woman may daydream about being with a man who will take complete care of her financially for the rest of her life, so she puts off educating herself. Such a woman gives no thought to the possibility that her future husband may become chronically ill, divorce her, lose his employment, or die.

Or there's the woman for whom mothering is the highest call. She doesn't see the importance of learning about finances because she is busy caring for her children and household. And yet most mothers handle money on a daily basis since they purchase groceries, gifts, clothing, and household items.

Some of us may be single and spend our money carelessly because we don't have anyone to whom we are accountable. We envision what we want and believe we deserve…and then spend accordingly.

Women who continue to daydream tend to have difficulty experiencing what is true and real. They often do not know where other people end and they begin. They become easily enmeshed in other people's ideas, beliefs, preferences, and emotions. They lean on others instead of on God. This leads to deception in all areas of their lives, including finances.

A woman's reality is a precious thing. It is her unique perspective or point of view about life as she experiences it through her spirit, body, mind, emotions, and behavior. If someone grew up in an emotionally unstable home, oftentimes it's hard to know what reality is. She may have trouble distinguishing her feelings and thoughts from those of her parents or other significant authority figures. These conflicts may show up in her behavior.

Women who have a distorted reality about their appearance or physical needs, for example, frequently deny themselves new shoes when the old ones are clearly worn out, avoid going to the dentist until they have an abscessed tooth or gum disease, or buy clothing only at thrift shops and bargain basements because they believe that's all they deserve. Daydreaming keeps women stuck.

We Believe in Holding onto Our Pain

Many of us act out our hurt instead of verbalizing it. We may rage at people without cause or pout or scream when we don't get our way. Maybe we shrink from any form of communication by simply leaving the scene.

Some women feel such intense emotional pain when it comes to discussing money that they cannot bear it. One of Kathy Miller's clients, for example, literally would leave the room whenever her husband wanted to talk about their finances. She had been raised in a family where her father took care of everything. She never had to think about money on any level. When her father died she couldn't handle the loss. So instead of *feeling* her grief, she went to the mall. She *decided* to become "clueless."

Miller believes, however, that women can move through grief and other pain in a relatively short span of time *if* they are willing to "feel it instead of acting it out." When we dramatize the hurt, we keep it alive and we keep ourselves immobile. We look for sympathy. We find people to whom we can relate our "story" again and again. We talk about our pain instead of *facing* it and *feeling it*. We invest an enormous amount of energy in trying *not* to feel, which actually makes us feel worse!

Only when we actually admit our pain and express it—through tears, sorrow, apology, regret—can we experience the comfort and healing that God provides and the renewal of energy He gives for whatever comes next.

We Believe We Shouldn't Have Needs

Many women ignore basic health care, nourishing food, exercise, sleep, privacy, prayer, even playtime because they believe they shouldn't have need of such things—or because they believe they don't deserve them. To keep this belief in place, these women have to work at it. But it takes energy to deny what is fundamental to their well-being, so they distract themselves by staying busy shopping, or gambling, or spending money frivolously. One woman said she had clothing in her closet with sales tags still on the sleeves, yet she claimed she didn't have enough money for teeth cleaning and a breast exam.

God has given us the gift of life, yet many of us take our bodies for granted or avoid taking care of them. One woman who is a midwife by profession has spent the last 35 years caring for women through their pregnancies and births, yet she admitted she has not had a routine pap smear herself in 18 years—despite all that she knows and all the advice she gives to others.

Women who deny themselves in such basic ways live as paupers even though money is available for the care they require. Perhaps they grew up in homes filled with chaos and drama around money, so they might have been ashamed of their appearance because their gym uniforms were never ready on the day they needed it, or their lunch always looked "funny" compared to those of their friends, or they never had a "cool" book bag like their schoolmates.

Today these beliefs are still in place. Though they are now adults, they cannot express their desire for a new car or a trip or a bouquet of fresh flowers without apologizing for it.

We Believe We Are Powerless

Many of us have been taught not to make a fuss, not to draw attention to ourselves, not to make waves. In essence, the message is: We are powerless. Stuffing our natural God-given power, however, takes enormous energy. When things begin to slip or a crisis occurs—such as a change in employment or a health problem with a family member—we may feel so "small" that we cannot ask for help even though help is all around us through friends, church groups, and community organizations that are designed to provide assistance.

God reminds us to ask and we will receive, but we don't hear that teaching. We allow fear, worry, or lack of self-care to keep us powerless and undeserving. Or we may tell ourselves that we *should* be able to handle things on our own. When we can't, then what? More energy is spent on hiding, protecting, or lying about what we need.

Many women also feel trapped when other people are in crisis around them. For example, a friend loses her job or has run up a credit card and needs a loan. You feel you *must* help her, regardless of how she got that way.

Some women have been discouraged from earning money and now feel powerless about how to manage it. Others feel powerless because they were forced to earn before they were ready, paying for items that were the responsibility of their caregivers. Still others may have been denied the opportunity to explore the world of work and earning because it brought a sense of shame or inadequacy to the parent in charge of income.

I remember wanting to babysit when I was about 12, but my parents needed me to sit for my younger sister and brother. To me that wasn't the same. They didn't pay me for the job. I wanted to earn money from what I considered to be a *real* babysitting job.

My friend Marlene, on the other hand, came from a broken family and *had* to work to help with groceries and rent. So her reality was also skewed. She was earning money for things that were her parents' responsibility to provide.

In a way, we were both powerless to express what was true for us at that pivotal stage in our development. It affected my ability to earn when the time came for me to do so, and it may have kept Marlene stuck in jobs that did not satisfy her true talent.

We Believe Cultural Lies

We've been taught as women that to get what we really want—acceptance, peace of mind, balance, love, well-being—we need to have husbands; trendy clothes and accessories; the "right" kitchen appliances; certain brands of furniture; golf, tennis, or gym membership; a great career; well-mannered, talented kids; and much more.

At the same time we are told to give to others without question, whether it's time and energy or personal belongings, and we should not ask or expect much in return. This is the ticket to friendship, approval, being part of the "in" crowd. What a burden for any woman to carry! The pressure to look good, behave appropriately, and essentially stuff true feelings is a lie that no one can swallow for long without destroying herself.

Such messages leave us feeling angry, confused, guilty, and ashamed. We know we can't be all things to all people at all times and still have a balanced and spiritually healthy life. So what is the truth, then?

The truth is found in Jesus…in his teachings. He did not mince words. He spoke plainly to anyone who was willing to listen and obey. He told us to love our brother (and sister) as we love ourselves. He taught us to seek first the kingdom of heaven and then the rest would be added. He told us to lean on him, not on our own understanding. And he told us to be still and know God. He also displayed these teachings in his own life. He went against the culture continually. He spent time with a prostitute, with lepers, with farmers and fishermen—clearly not the popular people.

He also drew away from the crowd when he needed to rest and pray. And he walked off when people were unwilling to hear what his Father had taught him. He reminds us not to throw pearls in front of pigs and to live in this world but not be of it. He does not tell us to compromise our integrity, but rather to surrender to his lordship.

I believe Jesus is telling us to focus on our own inner health first. Then we will have what we need to give to others, sharing from our abundance instead of from our lack. Living well as he taught us is no small thing. It takes courage to come against the cultural lies, to turn from false beliefs and behaviors, lazy thinking, and dependence on what other people think of us.

Believing God's Truth

Kathy Miller encourages women to find their hope in the Lord and in his rich promises found throughout the Bible. Here are a few of her favorite verses to meditate on as you renew your commitment to live an integrity-based life, anchored in God's truth.

> In everything set them an example by doing what is good. In your teaching show integrity... (Titus 2:7).

> What is impossible with men is possible with God (Luke 18:27).

> Now faith is being sure of what we hope for and certain of what we do not see (Hebrews 11:1).

> Do not be overcome by evil, but overcome evil with good (Romans 12:21).

> Let no debt remain outstanding, except the continuing debt to love one another, for he who loves his fellowman has fulfilled the law (Romans 13:8).

Each one should use whatever gift he has received to serve others, faithfully administering God's grace in its various forms (1 Peter 4:10).

Misfortune pursues the sinner, but prosperity is the reward of the righteous (Proverbs 13:21).

Then Jesus declared, "I am the bread of life. He who comes to me will never go hungry, and he who believes in me will never be thirsty" (John 6:35).

Taking Care of Ourselves

When we realize who we are in Jesus, we will recognize that we are equal to other people—not less than and not better than. That means it's okay and even the right thing to do to meet our basic needs for food, clothing, and shelter before we give to others. Meeting these needs requires sound financial practices. And sometimes for a woman to care for herself in a healthy way, counseling may be necessary to determine her needs realistically and to create a financial plan that works. Getting into financial shape also includes the following.

1. *Getting all of your financial information in front of you in one clear format.*

   Kathy Miller's workbook *A Good Steward's Journal: The Busy Christian's Guide to Better Money Management*[2] provides a practical approach to this step. Miller also recommends reading some of Suze Orman's materials for her clear presentations on financial planning. See the list of resources at the back of the book for more on this.

2. *Getting your time and space organized.*

   As you bring order to your environment and your day, your creativity will open up and you'll be able to accomplish things you only dreamed of before. For example, set aside one to two hours a week to record expenses, pay bills, and make a plan for the following week. This way you know exactly where you are financially and where you're headed. Get a notebook and record your dreams and goals. Note the amount of money needed to go on that trip you've dreamed about, go back to school, or purchase your own home. Plan accordingly! Visit www.organizingpro.com for some additional ideas.

3. *Getting rid of mental and emotional clutter.*

This includes old feelings, past beliefs, former behaviors that are no longer relevant to your life as an adult today. A coach, counselor, and/or an accountability or support group can help you get started on this internal house-cleaning. These may include Debtors Anonymous, Overcomers Outreach, Al-Anon family groups, or CODA (Codependents Anonymous)—all modeled after the original support program of Alcoholics Anonymous. (See Supplementary Resources at the back of the book for further information.)

4. *Getting your life in balance.*

Make time (don't wait for it to appear) for prayer and meditation, regular exercise, deep breathing, reflection, reading, and tithing (giving at least 10 percent of your earnings, no matter how small, to a charity or church or your choice). "When you're in survival, you can't share your gifts," says Kathy Miller. "It's essential to give to others even as you are giving to yourself. Tithing works for everyone. As you give you receive."

Richard Foster, in his book *The Challenge of Living the Disciplined Life: Christian Reflections on Money, Sex, and Power,* reminds us to earn all we can in order to take care of self and family first, then save, spend, and give away all we can. If we do that, then money does not become an end in itself. Ultimately money is not ours; rather, it's another one of the many blessings from God. Perhaps that recognition and acceptance is the most important realization we can have as we turn toward the restoration God has for us. But before we look at that, I'd like you to meet some women who have agreed to share their experiences, strengths, and hopes.

Part 2
Debt and
Dependence

3
A Woman's Place Is in the Mall— Overspenders

"I'd go to the mall every day if I could," said Kris. "Since I don't have to work, it gives me a place to go and a reason to get dressed in the morning. But I overspend. I know it, even though I'm not in debt. It feels good, but it also feels wrong, somehow."

Compulsive spending has interested Dr. Sharene Garaman for over a decade. It was the focus of her doctoral dissertation in clinical psychology and a specialty in her therapy practice. Originally from Wyoming, she lived and conducted her research in Southern California when I spoke with her.

As we sat in her living room overlooking a beautiful landscape, Garaman, dressed in jeans and a smart-looking lime-green shirt, talked about her commitment to learning all she can about the process of compulsive spending. People have told her that she is one of the few professionals they've met who really understands the problem. "Little wonder," she said laughing. "I began researching this subject initially for myself—I was a compulsive spender—and then because of my friends. I saw many of them doing with money what I had done."[1]

In professional literature, very little information or studies focus specifically on spending, unlike the large volume available on drug and alcohol abuse. Because of this, there is no clear, "official" definition of overspending. "We don't yet know how to define this behavior," Garaman said, "but we need a place to start. Some women, for example, believe that if they have an unlimited amount of money to spend and they're not in debt, then they're not compulsive spenders. But I think that's totally erroneous. There is more to the spending problem than simply being in debt."

Help with Behavior

Dr. Garaman favors a behavioral approach to treatment, partly because of what worked for her and what she found worked for her clients. "As a therapist I need to be able to tell my clients this is what I think and why, and this is what I do in this area. Then a woman can decide whether or not she wants to work with me. But if the entire subject is vague, you can't make any headway. I need to be able to help people change their behavior."

For example, if a client says she can't handle her money and is overspending regularly, Garaman feels it is important to help her "put the brakes on her behavior"—and not simply look at the reasons for spending. "The emotional issues are important, but that can come later in the recovery process. Down the road the woman will learn what her spending habits mean about her, but meanwhile she continues to spend, and probably will spend even more money because therapy itself produces anxiety."

One place to start analyzing your spending is to write down everything you spend money on. In her own life, Garaman says that listing her purchases was the single most important recovery tool she used. She didn't need a long-term emotional catharsis to discover the how and the why of spending. She just needed to see the evidence. "I was so appalled when I found out that I was spending 25 percent of my earnings on clothes that I stopped it right then. There was no getting around it. I just quit. Granted, I had to be at a point in my life where I could do that sort of thing."

Conspicuous Consumption

Therapy and group recovery programs sometimes focus on the personal and emotional levels of money abuse to the exclusion of the social and cultural influences. "We live in a very consumer-oriented society," Garaman comments. "And when you're defining compulsive spending, you have to take the culture into consideration. Not to do so would be incomplete.

"I come from Wyoming where spending is not as glamorized as it is here. I've never seen such conspicuous consumption anywhere as I have in Southern California. It gets to the point of vulgarity. When you're raised in this culture, I don't think spending is questioned to the degree it should be."

For example, "I was not a compulsive spender waiting to happen. My spending was precipitated by the culture. When I was 18 I went away to school and worked part-time at Joseph Magnin [a high-end department store]. Most of the clerks I knew spent a good deal of money in that store. They had credit cards—always maxed out—and it was accepted behavior."

She stopped for a moment, then continued, emphasizing her words. "I feel that's an important point," she added. "These people were older than I. They were my reference group—the ones I looked up to. If they did it, I thought I'd do it too. In addition, there was the pressure to look good."

Garaman paused, reflecting on that experience. "So did I have a lot of emotional needs that needed to be filled? Yes. But was that the reason why I spent my money? Initially, I think not." That early experience has had a great impact on the direction of her research and her work with overspenders. "In treating women with spending problems, I feel it would be jumping the gun to focus on the emotional issues alone."

Consuming Thoughts

Exploring the cultural influences may also involve looking at a woman's spiritual issues. For example, Garaman helps such women rethink their goals for their lives by exploring the answers to a number of questions: "Is this the way you want to live your life? Do you want to spend this much energy acquiring objects? Do you really need the latest everything? Is this a worthwhile lifestyle?"

Women who have unlimited resources are more difficult to reach because they don't think spending is an issue. "But," said Garaman, "I think they're in just as much trouble as those with a finite amount of money who get into debt because of their spending. Those who can't pay their bills are *more likely*, at some point, to wake up to their problem and do something about it.

"Part of the recovery process is to get women who overspend to step back and question their values and the culture's values around this kind of excessive spending. A lot of people still don't know that, however, because over-spending hasn't been defined." She pointed to the ongoing debate over alcoholism as a disease. "If researchers cannot even agree on a definition of the alcoholic after all that has been studied on this topic, then how can we expect to define a compulsive spender when there is so little research available?"

Ronnie is a good example of the kind of woman Garaman refers to. After graduating from college, Ronnie took a job in the fashion industry in Los Angeles. She and a friend got their own apartment and, of course, they were eager to fix it up. They didn't have money for everything they wanted since they were just starting their careers, so they began charging their purchases, believing they'd be able to pay off the balance each month as they got paid. But soon Ronnie's debts mounted. She felt she needed to look the part of a successful young businesswoman in L.A., a city famous for movie and television stars and sports and music celebrities who set the trends. So she charged clothing, jewelry, side-trips, manicures, hair-cuts, and makeup.

By the time she had accumulated $25,000 of credit-card debt she stopped paying attention to the number. When a friend invited her to dinner or a concert, she said yes without hesitation.

"I figured I was so far in debt by that time," she said, "one more night of fun wasn't going to make a difference one way or the other." But there came the day when she woke up and realized it was no longer $25,000, it was $70,000 spread over seven cards.

"I suddenly knew that I couldn't live this way another day. Everything changed in that moment. I was no longer willing to be obsessed about money. It had run my life morning and night."

She decided to meet with a credit counselor and create a plan to pay off the debt, no matter what it took—be it living in a smaller apartment, selling off some of her furniture, driving a used car, whatever. "I began to see the deception all around me, the lies I had bought into for years," she said with tears filling her eyes. "I was appalled and sickened by my own deceit as well. The things I called *mine* I did not own. The bank owned them. I got committed that day, and I've remained committed.

"I can't explain it, really. All I can say is that it was a spiritual act. Today, I'm proud to say that I am out of debt—and I did it without going into bankruptcy. I did it. I am eternally grateful for the wake-up call I received and for the grace to act on it."

Not All Money Abusers Look Alike

Some professionals believe that addiction is addiction, regardless of its expression. If you have deep-seated, unresolved emotional issues, then you are prone to addictive behavior—whether overspending, overeating, overworking, or drug or alcohol abuse. But this is a simplistic viewpoint. Lumping all addictions together and viewing all abusers as the same type of person just doesn't work. Sharene Garaman says it is valid and it can be helpful, however, to note some of the common characteristics of people who chronically overspend. In her experience these include:

> **Magical thinking.** Believing that needed money simply will appear from *somewhere*.

Projecting the "right" image. Spenders aren't stopped for spending, the way alcoholics may be stopped for drinking. Let's face it. A woman is not going to get pulled over to the side of the road for looking good, or for having too many Nordstrom sacks in her car!

Dressing well and being socially aware. Some of these women wear gold jewelry, makeup, and the most fashionable outfits even to the gym or grocery store.

Being concerned with how they are perceived by others. It is important to most women to look good and to be well thought of. One woman said she dressed to impress others and was aware that she did. Others say openly they want to model a certain actress or television star.

Spending on others. Some women justify their over-spending as valid because they see it as selfless. *They* don't deserve nice things but others do—so they spend on family and friends and employees. They are usually the ones who always find the perfect gift, regardless of the cost.

Wavering self-worth. Generally, women who think little of themselves, use spending as a way to feel. There's a distinction between compulsive shoppers and compulsive spenders. For example, Garaman says, "There are some women who wander the malls to the exclusion of other responsibilities, spending an inordinate amount of time shopping, whether or not they actually go into debt. The point is that they shop to avoid responsibilities. Then there are women who overspend but don't like to shop. They go into a store, spend their money, and leave. And of course there are those who shop and spend a lot of money and a lot of time."

Distinguishing Wants from Needs

Frequently women get into debt because they cannot distinguish their wants from their needs. One woman said she now sees that God has provided enough money for all her needs, but she keeps spending it on her wants! This is probably true of most of us. But distinguishing our needs from our wants can be a problem. Many overspenders don't know the difference. For example, "I went shopping with one of my best friends, who is a cruise director," said Garaman. "She wanted to buy a new evening gown. She had recently lost weight and was eager to purchase something that looked good on her. There were about four dresses she liked at $300 to $400 apiece.

"I shared with my friend one of my own realizations: We can't buy everything we look good in. But that was something of a revelation to my friend. She wanted all of them.

"I suggested she buy just one because she didn't really need four. I wanted to help her interrupt her overspending process. That day she bought just one. But the next day she sent someone from the ship to pick up the rest of the dresses.

"At that point she really believed that she *needed* all of them. Intellectually she knew differently, but emotionally she was sure she needed them."

Garaman has dealt with many women who struggle with the difference between a want and a need. "Actually, to subsist, there's very little we need," she added. "We all know the basics: food, clothing, and shelter. But women who don't see the difference between needs and wants actually talk themselves into believing that they really do *need* a $1500 leather coat."

In the following pages you'll meet three women—Julie, Suzanne, and Allison—who admit to confusion in their own lives about needs and wants. Each one has spent more money than she wants to and is facing the consequences of overspending. Maybe you can relate to their experiences.

The Class Clown: Julie's Story

"I hate malls. I hate shopping, and I don't like to try on clothes," said Julie, creator and president of a successful line of personalized gifts and novelty items that has recently gone nationwide. "I can go for a year without setting foot in a store."

Yet, Julie, like millions of other women, is an overspender. When she does shop she buys only the best…or the item with the most features or the highest price tag. "Apparently I think the more I spend, the better it is," she said, laughing.

When I asked her to share a little of her history regarding the subject of money, she tossed her head back and laughed again. "History, that's it. Whenever I have any money, it becomes history real fast."

I warmed up to her in seconds. She was open, easy to talk with, and quick-witted. I commented on her delightful sense of humor. "Humor has kept me going my whole life," she said, "through an uncertain childhood, through two failed marriages, through a recent encounter with breast cancer."

As a child, Julie was nominated the class clown. "I was truly a person who was laughing on the outside but crying on the inside," she said wistfully. The oldest of five children, Julie grew up in a two-bedroom bungalow in Detroit, Michigan. She remembers her father as a rageaholic—a person who was angry and suicidal his whole life. "I believe my dad was a genius," said Julie, but he was not educated so he never reached his potential.

"We never had enough money," she said. "He spent a lot of his earnings on food for himself. He was a 350-pound overeater who raided the refrigerator at night." Julie said this often meant the children went without milk and other breakfast food the next morning.

"We ate a lot of tuna casseroles in those days," she said, "and green beans. To this day I can't stand them. And I remember eating ring bologna."

Julie's mother was a quiet person who did not stand up to her husband. The understanding was that he earned the money, so he could spend it however he wished. But Julie said she also remembers her father as a generous person in his own way—as long as he was the one to decide how the money would be spent.

Julie said her mother would cower in the corner when her husband had a rage attack. But when he was away she released her feelings by yelling at the children. Julie believes that her own reckless attitude about life and her desire to take huge risks in relationships, with money, and with her business have resulted from her unstable upbringing.

"I was the black sheep in the family," she added. "I pulled all the pranks. Even my dad laughed at some of them. I've always lived on the edge. I was a sky-diver. I rode wild horses. I raced motorcycles. I even rode a motorcycle to work in downtown Detroit. I remember one day I knew I was going to be late for an important meeting, so I rode my motorcycle right into the building, took it on the elevator, and rode into the conference room. I got away with stuff like that. People expected it of me. They thought I was funny."

When Julie was a teenager she worked as a clerk at a variety store. "Every kid in the neighborhood looked forward to the day I got paid," she said. "They knew I'd bring them presents. I loved buying for others. It was a form of power and control."

But that changed when Julie got in with a popular group. "Many of the others had money," she said, "and I began to see the difference between them and me. Some of the girls snubbed me because I didn't have a cashmere sweater or Capezio shoes. I think that was the first time I made a real distinction between myself and others," she said with a catch in her voice, and then quipped, "Just when you catch up with the Joneses, they move."

Today, Julie is in debt—not a lot, but more than she's comfortable with. "I'm ready to change," she said. "I want to be well." She now keeps track of all her expenses—an important recovery tool suggested in the 12-step program Debtors Anonymous.

"I was shocked to find out that I spend about $200 a week on food," she added. "That's way too much for one person. But that's an indication of how I think. I usually buy the best-tasting or the most abundant whether in a grocery store or in a restaurant."

Even though Julie does not have heavy debts, she knows she's extravagant in ways that don't really satisfy her. She says she'd rather play "big shot" around other people, buying them gifts and meals, than take care of some of her real needs. Because she hates to shop and doesn't mind paying full price for her purchases, she tends to buy impulsively.

"I've spent nearly $300 on a three-month-old boy who's not even a relative. And I bought a $40 shirt for my employee's son just because I thought it was cute. It wasn't for any special occasion."

In addition, Julie said she gives away things without thinking. "If someone likes something I have, I give it to her. I also give away my time. At one point in my life I was volunteering up to 20 hours a week in addition to being a full-time real estate agent. I gave my blood. I gave out of guilt," she said soberly. "It seemed to help me deal with the shame of my childhood.

"I drive an 11-year-old car, and I haven't been to a dentist in 7 years. I went then only because it was an emergency. I haven't bought a business suit or a nice dress in the last 10 years. Most of the time I run around in painter's pants and a crummy T-shirt, playing the starving artist."

When Julie does shop, she's fast and precise. For example, after losing 50 pounds she decided to buy herself some new pants. "When I saw my size on the rack, I closed my hand over eight pairs at once, picked them up, and bought them. Yet I haven't worn some of them, and that was two years ago."

Another time Julie walked into a large chain variety store to buy some electrical tape. "One roll of black tape would have been fine," she said, "but no, I saw the various colors and decided I had to have two rolls of each color. I've never used them."

She says she has the same pattern with books. "If I see a book I like, I buy several copies—one for my car, one for the bedroom, one to read on the plane when I take a trip." Interestingly, her latest multiple-book purchase was one on how to get out of debt.

Julie also has a surplus of 200 drawer dividers, the result of another overspending spree. Her spending patterns and rituals are humorous on the surface, but to Julie they're not funny anymore. The pain of overspending and taking care of herself has caught up with her, and she's working seriously now at changing her patterns.

To the Manor Born: Suzanne's Story

"From the beginning my parents were mismatched," said Suzanne, a genteel, slow-speaking woman in her mid-sixties. "My mother was terminally vague. My father made split-second decisions. So they never got together on anything."

Suzanne, the last of three children, was born when her parents were in their forties. They had lost their firstborn and almost lost Suzanne's sister to scarlet fever. "So I was raised delicately, raised to be spared," said Suzanne.

"My mother was a victim of what I call vignette thinking," she said. The term fascinated me, and I asked her to explain. "She never saw the big picture. She'd see a dress or a pair of earrings or a painting, and immediately it would remind her of something else—some other time or experience, or it might be something she never had. She'd have to have it for my sister or me. She'd obsess about it until she bought it. We had everything we ever wanted and more. She also pushed us ahead of our time—especially my sister. For instance, my mother wanted her to date before she was ready."

Suzanne believes that some of her financial excess was also due to the fact that her parents were older and had less energy for two active girls than younger people might have had. Therefore, it was easier to give their daughters *things* than to give them their time. "They never set limits because they didn't want any stress. I could have anything I wanted."

One thing Suzanne wanted was to wear braids and be a tomboy. "I was allowed to be a tomboy," she said, reflecting on her early years, "but

I also had to take ballet lessons." She also received a horse, riding lessons, and attended the finest schools.

Suzanne truly felt that she was "to the manor born." But as she grew up, she found the world was not as hospitable or as eager to take care of her as her parents had been. "I remember I couldn't be around fast-moving people," she said, drawing out each word in soft, cultured tones. "For the first time in my life I began to feel less than others. I couldn't get organized that quickly."

Like her mother before her, she married a man who could make decisions quickly and keep her and her sons in tow. He was a career officer in the Navy, so once again, Suzanne lived in an environment where she was totally cared for. The Navy compound provided everything she needed. As a result, Suzanne admits, she never learned how to live in the real world.

But amid the pampering and the plenty, her life was not without tragedy. Her only sister committed suicide at age 38, and Suzanne's husband died while she was in her mid-thirties. She was then faced with rearing her three boys alone. "I had so much stress trying to keep order during those years that I didn't want any more. So, like my parents, I never set any boundaries for my sons. And I have no boundaries in my life. All three of my boys have problems to this day because of it. In fact, our entire family has a history of mental illness. It seems to be generational."

In the late 1980s, Suzanne put her family house on the market and planned to purchase a $300,000 condominium for herself and one of her sons who lives with her. But that purchase didn't work out, so she decided on a $500,000 house.

Reflecting on that time, she said with dismay, "Can you imagine? In a split second I jumped my expenditure by $200,000 without thinking, planning, or consulting anyone."

For years Suzanne had listened faithfully to Bruce Williams, a financial advisor on talk radio, yet when it came to making such an important decision as buying and selling a house, she did so without an attorney, CPA, or financial planner. "I did it on my own, and everything about it was wrong. The house is like a boat that has been under water for 50 years!"

For the first couple of years Suzanne put an enormous amount of money into fixing it up and restoring it instead of selling it. She says she's aware now that obsessing about the house took her mind off paying attention to the real problems in her life.

"I blank out when it comes to money," she admits. "I've spent a lot of money on a gardener for a house that's not even fit to live in. And I'm a soft touch for everyone else's needs. The gardener gave me a story about needing a new tire for his truck, so I bought him one. And on it goes.

"I see that I participate in unsatisfying activities to keep my mind off my pain. I remember hearing someone on a talk show saying that our activities take us away from the boredom of our own gray, deprived lives. That's absolutely true of me. I waste so much time and energy.

"For example, one summer one of my sons and his family said they might come and stay with me a few nights. It was not definite, but that didn't matter to me. I went in to a whirlwind of spending. I didn't have room for them in my condo so I decided to put them up at *the* house. It was empty—no furniture—and they could have used sleeping bags for the two nights, and then spent the days with me at the condo. But no, I was raised to think that guests in your home are little gods. So I spent $1,500 to $2,000 on beds and bedding so they'd have comfortable places to sleep. The beds are still there, the house hasn't sold, and my son's family never came."

One year she was invited to New York to attend the wedding of her cousin's daughter. "My cousin knows my financial situation," she said, "and made a point of telling me not to buy anything, just to come, that my presence would be a gift in itself. But no, I got over-elated and went on a spending spree, buying more gifts than I could afford. I spent another $2,000 than was necessary. In fact, my cousin told me that the family silver, which I had intended to give her daughter, was more than enough. But I couldn't accept that. I had to make the silver look good. So I took it to a professional and had every piece burnished, costing me $250 or so."

This was another attempt, Suzanne claims, to keep her mind off what's really important. "When my father died he left me $86,000," Suzanne added.

"I lost $50,000 of it in investment scams. I didn't have top advisors helping me so I got into things I didn't investigate or fully understand."

Suzanne said she also overspends on intangible items, such as long-distance phone calls. "They're safe," she said. "I call people so they won't come over and see my junk or my moods."

Suzanne is now taking steps toward becoming responsible, however, through a 12-step program, a women's group, and a Bible study at her church. "I still struggle," she said, "but I also see small changes."

Plain Jane: Allison's Story

While Allison was growing up, she never had money of her own. Nor did her parents have money to spend on the pretty things she admired in the lives of school friends. She was raised in a lower-middle-class family and though she had been well cared for she knew that fashionable clothes, a new bicycle, or a special trip were for *others,* never for her.

"I thought of myself as a 'plain Jane,'" she said. "Inside I felt creative and I loved to have fun, but I had few opportunities to express myself. I used to daydream about what it would be like to dress in trendy clothes and have the latest shoes." Allison never felt her clothes matched her personality. She spent time thinking about the kind she'd buy if she had enough money, and she entertained herself by drawing pictures of the outfits she admired. "I always had what I needed," she admitted, "but rarely what I wanted. "

Her parents were kind and hardworking. They provided a secure environment and a happy family life full of traditions and celebrations. Despite these comforts, Allison felt different from the other girls at school. "I was envious and discontent," she said. "And these feelings stayed with me into my adult life."

Allison later married a man with a modest income. They had a good marriage and looked forward to family life together. Allison worked full-time and could spend her income as she pleased because of their affordable rent and low monthly overhead. But when Allison had her first child, she stopped working.

"For the first time since we were married, I felt squeezed financially," she said. "I was used to buying what I wanted when I wanted," she added with a playful laugh. "I had gotten spoiled, and I enjoyed it."

Allison said she had never gone overboard, but she liked having something cute and new to wear to work each day. Then suddenly she was restricted to a small allowance out of her husband's salary. Shopping was no longer *fun*. It became a chore to stay within their budget.

All that changed, however, when Allison came into a large sum of money—*the hard way*. At age 33, when her daughter was two years old, Alison had an accident at the gym where she worked out regularly. It caused a severe injury to her hand, and led to a sizable settlement from the defendant's insurance company.

When she received the check she began shaking all over. "I was holding a check payable to me for $75,000," she said. "I had never seen that kind of money at one time. Friends told her she should have sued the gym and received more. They felt she had settled for too little. After all, her hand was permanently injured.

Allison, however, couldn't have imagined more. "It already seemed like more than I could handle," she added, breathing deeply as she described the feeling of exhilaration that came over her.

Family members advised her about investing safely. She was interested in what they had to say but couldn't quite put it into action. She had never expected such a windfall, and she didn't want to make a hasty decision. Although Allison admitted she didn't know anything about how to manage the money, she felt sure it would last forever.

She deposited the check into her bank account and decided then to treat herself to something special after all the pain and trouble she had suffered. She bought an expensive outfit and took four of her closest friends to dinner at a high-end restaurant. Then she traded in her old car for a new one, using part of the settlement as the down payment on the auto loan, updated the master bathroom, and took a trip. By then she had spent $20,000 but was hardly aware of the number at the time. She did not keep track of the savings account, but she wasn't worried because she believed she was finished spending. She was determined not to withdraw any more of the money.

But her good intentions did not last long. Over the next two years, Allison spent every last penny. It dribbled away as she and her daughter spent their days having lunch out and shopping.

She wrote checks for her purchases since her husband was adamantly opposed to credit cards. Every few days she looked at her checking account balance and was shocked at the low figure. She handled that by transferring funds from her savings account to her checking account.

"I told myself that I would put it back on payday," she said with a wistful tone, "but it never happened. My husband's check was never enough to cover bills *and* my withdrawals."

By then Allison was in a habit that was hard to break. "I knew deep down that I was using some of the money for frivolous things, but I didn't want to stop so I just ignored the numbers. I couldn't imagine that I had used up more than a couple thousand at the most."

She had no idea at the time that she was burning through the remaining $55,000 on lunches, coffee lattes, shoes, and flea-market finds. "I was physically ill," she said, "when I had to face what I had done. My husband had no idea. He never paid attention to what I was bringing home. Maybe he figured I was just good at making our household allowance stretch."

Allison said that telling her husband was the hardest thing she ever had to do. He was hurt and angry. He didn't speak to her for two days. He couldn't believe how irresponsible she had been. He had viewed that money as their nest egg.

Allison has since recovered from this humiliating experience, and she learned an important lesson in the process. "What you can't face, you can't fix," she said. "I spent money in order to avoid feeling the pain of the accident, the permanent damage I've sustained, and of having lived for so long with so little of what I really wanted."

Today Allison has a good job as a secretary with a salary she can live with. "I bank a certain percentage each week," she said, "and my husband and I discuss all purchases before we make them. I still like fashionable clothing, but I realize I no longer *need* 10 T-shirts and 6 pairs of jeans and 12 pairs of shoes. And I can get along just fine with one coffee latte a week!"

But most of all, Allison credits God with her change. "He has seen me through the toughest of times. I know he will sustain me for the rest of my life. I am now leaning on his guidance, not on my own compulsions."

Taking Inventory

Women who are overspenders answer "often" or "very often" to many of these statements:

1. I buy things I don't really need or want.

2. If I have money in my purse I feel I have to spend it.

3. I buy things even when I cannot afford them.

4. I spend money to make myself feel better.

5. I overspend on gifts to impress or gain the approval of others.

6. I buy things on sale just because they're on sale.

7. I indulge in spending rituals such as buying in pairs.

8. I feel secretive about my spending habits.

4
Born to Shop— Shopaholics

My Aunt Meg fascinated me as I was growing up. She had the ability to produce, seemingly from nowhere, bathing suits of every size and color, blouses and shorts, socks and scarves. When she gave me a gift for a birthday or graduation, she urged me to slip into it right on the spot. If it was the wrong size or color or a style I didn't like, no problem. She'd fly off to one of the back rooms and return in an instant with a replacement. Or if she were visiting at our house, she'd run out to the car and do the same.

She apparently kept a stock of items on hand for all occasions and for all the people in her life. She had a family of six children and numerous nieces, nephews, sisters, in-laws, and friends. There was always someone to give something to. I don't recall the gifts ever being wrapped; they were just handed over. Her generosity pleased me, and her willingness to produce the perfect item each time continues to fascinate me.

I don't know if Aunt Meg was born to shop or if she was simply a generous person who enjoyed shopping for family and friends. But I do know that she spent many hours poring over sales and buying items in bulk.

I also remember hearing stories about the mother of one of my childhood friends who went shopping *every day*. It was as much a part of her routine as cooking or gardening. She said it helped her relax. My friend was one of the best-dressed kids in our sixth-grade class. I had one pair of school shoes. She had four. I had one bathing suit. She had two or three. When we met again years later, I asked her if her mother was still shopping. Her face sobered when she told me that her parents had gotten divorced while she was in college. Her mother had run up so much debt that they lost the family home and, in the end, filed for bankruptcy. My friend said she has the same problem with shopping, but when she saw it getting a grip on her life she got into counseling before she lost her family too.

A Serious Problem

There is shopping for food and clothing, a car and a house in order to live. And there is living in order to shop—the kind of shopping where your heart beats faster as you approach the front door of your favorite department store. Some women go on a shopping binge for several days and then abstain for months. Others shop as a form of entertainment. They don't go into debt, but they enjoy walking through a mall and buying a few things as much as other women might enjoy a hike in the mountains or a couple of sets of tennis.

I sense that my Aunt Meg fit somewhere in the middle. She spent a lot of money on stuff, but usually it was for other people. Somehow that made it respectable—even admirable. And my schoolmate's mother… well, by today's definition she would be considered a compulsive shopper.

Shopping and women, women and shopping. The perfect marriage. They go together like a horse and carriage. And our culture blesses the union. Women are expected to shop, encouraged to shop, wooed into shopping. That's a huge part of the problem. Even the term *shopaholic* is a cutesy take-off on the word *alcoholic*. But there is nothing cute about compulsive shopping. It is a serious addiction for millions of women, every bit as serious as drug, alcohol, or food abuse.

According to author Conny Jasper in an article entitled "Addicted to Shopping," "Never before in history has there been so many different things to buy, or so many places to buy things from....All around us are constant opportunities to purchase every kind of bauble, gadget, or toy. And in spite of dire predictions about the current economy, American people are still shopping with a passion. As comedian George Carlin once joked onstage, 'Home is where you keep your stuff, so that you can go out and buy more stuff.' Even after the September 11th terrorist attacks, Americans were encouraged to go out shopping in order to show their support for the 'American way of life.' "[1]

Compulsive shopping is particularly insidious because, unlike dark alley dysfunctions such as drugs and alcohol, shopping is pristine.

Maria, a compulsive shopper, says she *has* to shop in order to feel good. "It's the *shopping* itself that I like. It doesn't matter what I buy. In fact, the things I buy usually look great in the store, not so good the next day, and a week later they look awful."

Maria sighed deeply and folded and unfolded her slender hands. "But I still do it. Then I hate myself and feel guilty. And to get rid of those feelings I go shopping again. It's one sick cycle, I know. But I can't seem to break it, no matter how many times I promise myself that this will be the last time. I have clothes in my closet that I've never taken out of the bags. The tags are still on a pair of pants I bought two years ago. Why don't I take the stuff back? I don't know. That's not fun. It's a hassle, and the clerks look at you like you're trying to rob their commission or something. Besides, what I really like is shopping, not returning things."

Shopping addiction hits hard among young women. Our culture creates such a hunger for things. Just watching Oprah makes a woman want new stuff, especially on the day when she displays her "favorites"—from pajamas to body lotions. But shopaholics span all age groups. One 87-year-old woman has gone through $150,000 in three years because she can't stop shopping. Confined to her home because of arthritis, part of her entertainment is the Internet.

Any woman can find a reason to justify a day at the mall, a quick stop at a boutique, a few items from the mail-order catalog, or an afternoon in front of the shopping channel. Every woman needs clothes and equipment for work and school and sports and evenings out. Then there are gifts for others, the right car, and of course, the perfect accessory. Shopaholics are decent women—women who care about how they look and how they feel…but to an extreme.

A System of Shoulds

Most shopping addicts are living out someone else's "should system"— their mothers', a celebrity's, a manufacturer's, a designer's, a friend's. They are dealing with psychological and social influences so great they cannot even consider them, much less face and deal with them. Issues of low self-worth, lack of boundaries, and problems with reality are all part of the complex behavior that plays itself out in a shopping frenzy.

Even our language supports this system of addiction. Cars boast bumper stickers such as "When the going gets tough, the tough go shopping" or "I'd rather be shopping." "Born to shop" is emblazoned on a coffee mug one of my daughters received as a gift. Even the expression "shopping spree" suggests out-of-control buying. In addition, stores encourage shopping by featuring cafes and snack bars on the same floor as popular merchandise. Customers are invited to open a charge account so they can acquire a preferred rating. Personal shopping services are available for women who want a professional clothing consultant to help coordinate a wardrobe or a special outfit.

None of these services of itself is bad. Some of them are even helpful and certainly convenient. I have enjoyed hiring a personal shopper, and when I did use department store credit cards I found them a wonderful convenience. I could do all my shopping in one day, in one place, without having to write individual checks in each department. At the end of the month I'd write one check for the entire purchase and bring my balance back to zero. That worked for me because compulsive shopping is not my problem.

But to a person who is easily addicted, the colors, textures, jewelry, books, clothing, and cosmetics in a row of stores and boutiques are as seductive as potato chips to an over-eater. Bet you can't buy just one. Compulsive shopping has been the cause of marriages breaking up, bankruptcy, theft, and a host of other maladies that suck the very life out of the women who drop by the mall "to pick up a few things."

Compulsive shopping is not just the domain of those who wish to keep up appearances or those who are material minded. There are shopaholics of every nationality, background, and belief system. Women with strong spiritual convictions are just as likely to be found pounding the pavement of a mall as someone who believes in living just for today.

One Christian woman said she justifies her shopping addiction by limiting herself to Christian bookstores and church thriftshops. "I buy books and bumper stickers and music tapes and T-shirts for my grandkids and greeting cards and on and on. As long as it's got a spiritual angle, I find a way to rationalize buying it. But now that I'm in Overcomers Outreach— a Christian support group for people with addictions—I see how much I've been kidding myself."

Kim Hong moved with her family to the United States from Vietnam during the mid-1970s when she was 15. She remembers being overwhelmed by the large supermarkets and grocery stores. "At first I was afraid to go shopping," she said. "But now I'm a—what do you call it—shopaholic. I want everything I see. We were very poor when I was growing up and, of course, in Vietnam during the war years, we didn't have the opportunity to do anything but survive."

Now in her mid-thirties, Kim has her own beauty salon, her own money, and her own life. "It's as though I am trying to make up for all those years when I had nothing, not even a pair of shoes. But it is so easy in this country to go into debt. I think it's wrong. Now I am working hard to pay back what I owe—$10,000. Even though I owe so much money,

I still find things I want to buy. I love to shop. The stores here are so beautiful."

Filling the Void

There are as many ways to shop compulsively as there are women who do it. But one thing most appear to have in common is a need to fill the emptiness they feel inside. One 32-year-old executive secretary in Beverly Hills reported that the night before Valentine's Day one year she and her boyfriend had a fight. She knew there would be no flowers or candlelight dinner for her the next day.

"That morning my feelings of anger and resentment were so strong all I could think to do was shop. 'If he doesn't love me, then I can love myself,' I thought. During my lunch hour I marched right over to Rodeo Drive and charged a $1,000 watch I had been wanting for months. Then I walked back to work as if I had just bought a $10 bracelet."

Another compulsive shopper said she spends her money on other people to keep relationships going. "I have a birthday book that rivals the Yellow Pages," she said, laughing. "I'm absolutely nutty about remembering people's birthdays. I spend so much money on Hallmark products they ought to make me a stockholder. I lose all sense of reality in a stationery store. I pick up cards like most people pick up groceries. It's nothing for me to drop $50 at a time."

Anxiety, depression, competition, insecurity in relationships, and stress on the job are common factors that trigger compulsive shopping. But the roots of these feelings are much deeper, as shown in the stories of the following four women.

The Fur Muff: Georgia's Story

Georgia learned early in life that money could stimulate her emotions. Her father was a traveling salesman for a book company. When sales were up, he'd come home with presents for everyone. "I especially remember a little brown fur muff he gave me to warm my hands," said Georgia, a tall, slender brunette. "I was about seven at the time, and it was the most wonderful present I could ever imagine. It was all the more special because my dad picked it out just for me."

But when sales were down and commissions low, so were her father's emotions. "He'd come in the door and barely speak to any of us. Then my mother would scurry around shushing us kids and waiting on Dad hand and foot, trying to win him back. I went right along with her. But when I think of it now, it makes me sick. He ran the show from the road. Today he'd be considered an absentee father. And yet his power over our household was so strong, you'd think he was there 24 hours a day."

Georgia, in an interesting re-creation of her past, also works in sales. Single at 48, she lives out of a suitcase most of the time and spends many hours alone, driving from one city to another. At night she often eats by herself, then ends her day walking through a mall.

"If I'd just browse, it'd be fine," she said. "But it never stops there. I always find something I absolutely have to have. I'm never bored because I'm in different cities several days a month.

"To me a shopping mall is like a carnival," said Georgia. "I get absolutely high with the colors and textures and displays. Clothes are my downfall. I have enough to start my own boutique," she said, laughing in embarrassment. "In fact, my best friend tells me I ought to start a resale clothing store since my own stock could keep me going for a year," she said, with a catch in her voice.

"If it weren't so pathetic, I'd laugh—and maybe even consider it. But it's not funny anymore. I'm a shopping junkie. I've gotten over my food addiction, and I no longer drink. But I can't stop shopping.

"I also have a thing about being on mailing lists. I sign up at every store. It makes me feel important to be a preferred customer, to be one of the people who hears about the sales and promotions before the rest of the world. I guess it's like the feeling I had when my dad gave me the fur muff. I was special. I had a muff before any of my friends had one."

Georgia's mother was a quiet person, but she, too, loved to shop. When things got steamy around the house, her mother rounded up the girls—Georgia and her two sisters—and took them shopping on Mason Avenue, a street in their town lined with shops and boutiques, five-and-ten-cent stores, and ice cream parlors.

"My mother would buy us each a little something—maybe a bow for our hair or a new pair of socks 'to cheer you up,' she'd say. Then we'd stop for a soda or ice cream. Afterward we went home, and things seemed calmer somehow. I think I began to associate shopping with feeling good and with taking away the loneliness I felt so much of the time while growing up."

Today, Georgia owes $15,000 to department stores and credit-card companies. She's seeking help from Consumer Credit Counselors. "I feel hopeful for the first time in my life," she said, flashing her deep-brown eyes. "I need help, and I'm willing to receive it."

Never Enough: Ann's Story

Ann's shopping addiction is also rooted in her childhood. She was the only girl and eldest of six children. "My parents were ultraconservative fundamentalist Protestants, and my father believed a woman's place was in the home, at least while the children were young." The fact that he earned very little as a college professor did not change his view.

Ann's mother continued to get pregnant because "she believed it was God's will" despite the fact that her health was fragile. "That meant she was confined to bed at the beginning of the second trimester of each pregnancy to prevent premature birth. It also meant that I reared my brothers.

"In looking back," Ann said, her blue eyes misting as she spoke, "there are two indelible messages about money that came from my childhood.

One, there is never enough, and two, my ticket to high-level earning power was a college education. So I grew up believing that all I had to do was earn a degree and at graduation I would get a huge salary!"

Ann was not taught how to manage money in any way she could understand. "When I asked my mother for things any normal child would want, such as a doll or a bicycle or a special dress like my friends had, she would take me to the desk where she paid our family bills, show me the numbers on the expense sheet, what my father earned, and where it went," said Ann. "This may have been a reasonable teaching tool for an older child, but I was only five or six at the time.

"She told me that if I could find the money for a bicycle or new doll I could get it—but then she'd remind me that if I got something that meant my brothers would have to do without." The message Ann received was clear: You'll never get anything you ask for. There is no way to have anything you want. "I was too young to earn money, and there was no allowance. By age seven, I stopped asking for anything."

One positive thing she remembers is her parents' absolute accountability for debts. With six children there were always unexpected expenses, but her mother and father made certain they all had adequate medical and dental care, food, clothing, and housing. "The bills were always paid, though sometimes a small amount at a time. I learned that a debt incurred was a debt to be paid.

"I started babysitting when I was 12 to earn extra money," she continued. "I could use whatever I earned for my personal expenses. I remember using it all for impulse buying. I never saved anything. I felt very grown-up to be able to get whatever I wanted. I did, however, make certain that what I wanted would fit the amount of money I had. That pattern still exists today."

Ann married after she graduated from college and found out later that her husband was a practicing alcoholic, womanizer, and debtor. She worked hard to pay off his debts to avoid the fear and shame they brought on. After years in this dysfunctional environment, her marriage ended when she discovered her husband had forged her name on several credit union loans.

Following the divorce, Ann admits to going totally nuts. She began taking trips to see friends out-of-state and charging the airline tickets. "Of course, I had to have clothes for each trip. I bought $2,000 to $3,000 worth of stuff, and I've continued to spend money on lunches, clothes, pieces of art, books, and fabric that I never make into anything." Ann's shopping was compulsive at times, but she always made a point of finding things that "wouldn't get me into trouble later, or something that I could hide easily. For example, earrings. I think I have 200 pairs. None of them is expensive. When I'd feel down, I'd buy a new pair of earrings." Unlike most shopaholics, Ann fits the purchases to her budget. But that can be as deceptive as spending too much. "I'm never clear about what I really want because I don't make a list or set a goal or plan for big purchases."

Since there was never enough as a child, Ann has no real-life experience with planning or saving. At one time she did manage to save $3,000, but then she was laid off from her job and had to use all but $500 of it. "I still have that $500. I think of it as my own, and it feels good."

Ann said she also has some unusual shopping habits. For example, "after hosting an elegant formal dinner party at my house one night," she said, "the next day I *had* to go out and buy 12 soup bowls to go with my good china." She had to have the bowls, she said, because at the party the night before she was forced to use bowls from her everyday set.

"I remember my heart pounding while I made the purchase," said Ann. "I knew it wasn't necessary, and yet I *had* to have them." She had planned on getting the soup bowls only, but when she saw they were on sale, the clerk suggested she buy the fruit dishes too. "And then I added a soup tureen since it was such a good price! I spent $300 to $400, yet I've never used any of them.

"For me, money is not just something you use to purchase something. It is pain and shame and anxiety and lack of clarity about what I want and what I need and how to get them. I recently realized, in recovery, that I also grew up thinking that *my* money was play money for whatever I wanted. The *real* money—for food and clothing and survival—came from the men in my life."

Today Ann is sorting out her wants and needs and coming to terms with her fear and shame around finances. She's unraveling the distorted messages she received about God's teachings on money. She regularly attends meetings of Debtors Anonymous.

I'll Take Two: Esther's Story

Esther believed at one time that she was born to shop. She liked to joke about it. But unlike Georgia and Ann, Esther buys in pairs. "I can *never* buy just one of anything," said the brunette in her late thirties. "I remember shopping with my Jewish grandmother who raised me, and she always bought more than one—from bagels to chickens," she said.

"She had what I call an emergency philosophy. She was always preparing for a crisis. If I were buying a candy bar, she'd say, 'Buy two, honey, in case you get hungry later.' If I saw a blouse or skirt I liked, she'd urge me to get two—one for good wear and one for everyday, or one for now and one for later. She planned ahead to the point of obsession. 'What if it breaks or gets lost or somebody steals it?' she'd ask. 'You'll have a second one, and you won't worry.' "

Esther said this compulsive process drove her crazy. They had two can openers, two toasters, two cookie jars, and so on. Later, when Esther was living on her own, she found herself shopping in the same compulsive way. Debt was not as much of a problem for her as the ritual of shopping for pairs.

"You should see my house," she said, laughing self-consciously. "You wouldn't believe the collection of weird stuff I have. Two cans of paint, when one is enough; two sets of dishes, though I live alone; two irons; two this, two that. I hate it, but somehow I feel incomplete if I buy just one of something. I find myself remembering my grandmother's warning that I'll be sorry if I have only one and it breaks or gets lost or is stolen.

I have so much junk I wish someone would steal a few things. I don't use half the stuff I buy."

Esther's ritualistic shopping also stands in the way of planning or saving for anything meaningful. "For example, I've never taken a real vacation since I started working over ten years ago. And I don't have any play clothes. I recently discovered while sharing in my therapy that I don't have these things because I think I don't deserve to play. With a crisis just around the corner, who has time for fun? That realization was a real breakthrough for me.

"My grandmother believed in hard work, nose-to-the grindstone kind of thing. Even though shopping was an outlet for her, she bought only things that made sense to her—and then she bought two so she'd never be without."

Esther finds she has the same odd mixture of values. "I buy serviceable items—in pairs, of course," she said, laughing. "But they never really satisfy me. And because I buy two of everything, I don't have enough money to buy something I really want—like a pure silk blouse or a genuine leather purse."

Esther, like other compulsive shoppers, is also a woman in debt. "It's not a lot by most standards, but it's crippling *me*," she said, poking herself in the chest as if to make a point, "especially the interest payments. I feel like I'll be paying for can openers and plastic potato chip bag clips for the rest of my life. I can't seem to leave a mall without charging something or using up every bit of money I have in my wallet."

She shifted her gaze for a moment and then continued softly as if to apologize. "I rarely buy big items like a lamp or a chair or a bed. I fritter away my money on little things. That's how I keep myself in a rut. Then, when a friend invites me to a movie or to go away for a weekend, I tell her I can't afford it. The truth is I don't think I deserve to take a day off when I have so much debt. I should be working to pay it off."

No More Hand-Me-Downs: Roberta's Story

Roberta, a beautiful Hispanic woman of 39, was born in Los Angeles, the last of six children. "We never lacked for food," she said. "But I never had many clothes, and most of what I did have were hand-me-downs from my older sisters. My dad was a workaholic and an alcoholic. And he was very tight with his money, except when it came to my mother. He bought her many gifts—new cars, expensive jewelry—and he had her clothes made for her."

Because her father was the dominating one in the family, Roberta grew up depending on him. She never learned to take care of herself. Whenever she and her siblings needed anything, they had to ask their dad for it and justify why it was necessary. "I grew up expecting others to take care of me," she admitted. "I never learned to save, never planned for the future or for my retirement."

As an adult, when she spent money on herself Roberta felt wonderful. "I saw it as a way of taking care of myself," she said. "I also spent it so I wouldn't have to share it. No matter how much I had, I'd get rid of it. I was afraid to buy anything tangible or I might have to share it with someone else." Instead, she bought consumable items such as books, airline tickets, and gifts.

Roberta married twice. "I married the first man because I knew he'd be a good provider, and I'd be secure. But I didn't love him." She soon discovered that he had all the characteristics of her father. "He was traditional, tight with money, and very controlling. I hid all my purchases from him."

Eight years after her divorce, Roberta married again. "It was for love," she said. "He was an artist, and I thought it would be different this time. In a way it was. In this relationship he was the debtor. I had reversed the roles. He was looking for someone to take care of him!"

Roberta had credit cards, and she let him use them. After two years they divorced, and she was left with $12,000 of debt. "He ruined my credit," she said, "and I was forced to step down in my life. I moved to a dinky apartment in order to save enough money to pay back the debts."

But Roberta discovered after her second divorce that her own problem with shopping and spending was not over. Her cycle of debt erupted again. "I knew my income, and I was uncomfortable with how much I spent." Roberta buys clothes, presents, meals, and odds and ends she doesn't really need—anything to keep the money out of her hands and away from her bank account. "I have used shopping and spending as proof that I can take care of myself."

Over the years Roberta has stopped her compulsive shopping for as much as five years at a time, but eventually she returned to it. This stop-and-start mode is a family pattern, she admits. "My father did the same thing with alcohol," she said. "He'd stop for a time and then start again.

"I've always had this desire to be special in my family," she said. "Shopping, spending, charging on credit cards gave me a sense of power."

Today Roberta is engaged to be married again, and she admits that she has a lot of fear about the marriage, as well as money. "We went to look at rings," she said, "and that shopping experience sent me on an emotional roller coaster. I realized how things can sneak up on me if I'm not aware and conscious of each moment. A week after I received the ring, my fiancé came over and basically said, 'Where's dinner?'" Roberta laughed at the implication. The old male/female dynamic dies hard.

Today she is looking at her fear and some of the messages she received in parochial school and from her parents who were very controlling. At the invitation of a friend, she decided to join a Bible study to find out what God's Word has to say about money and marriage and some of the other concerns she has.

Taking Inventory

Women who are compulsive shoppers answer "often" or "very often" to many of these statements.

1. Shopping is my most common form of entertainment.

2. I feel anxious when I am not shopping.

3. Shopping takes the place of talking and feeling and dealing with the unpleasant realities of my life.

4. I argue with others about my shopping and spending habits.

5. I repeatedly buy things I neither need nor want.

6. I get a rush or a high from the shopping process or even just thinking about it.

7. I am concerned about how often I shop, but I continue to shop anyway.

8. When talking to others, I minimize my purchases or hide them.

9. I buy clothing that does not fit my lifestyle—business suits or heels—when I rarely, if ever, use them.

5
Maxed Out—
Credit-Card Abusers

Credit cards are as foreign to Gina's present lifestyle as hamburgers are to a vegetarian. But it was not always that way. At one time Gina owed nearly $25,000 in credit-card debt. She had three bank cards and two department store cards, and each one was maxed out. It took her five years at a second job to pay off the debt.

"I'll never put myself through that again," she said, despite the fact that the creditors continue to entice her with new cards and higher limits because of her "excellent record." Gina knows differently now. The credit-card companies are not as interested in her payment performance as they are in the interest they earn on her installments.

When she purchased a winter coat for $250 at a large department store in Manhattan, for example, the clerk rang up the sale and asked, "May I put this on your credit card?" Gina declined, saying she preferred to pay cash. She handed the clerk three $100 dollar bills. But the clerk did not have sufficient change on hand, so she called customer service to have it delivered to her department.

"I never thought I'd see the day when cash was more of a hassle than credit," said Gina.

Credit-Card Mania

According to Liz Pulliam Weston, columnist for MSN Money Central,

- ❋ More than a third—36 %—of those who owe more than $10,000 on their cards have household incomes under $50,000, according to the VIP Forum analysis.
- ❋ 13% who owe that much have household incomes under $30,000.
- ❋ The percentage of disposable income used to pay debts is still near record highs.
- ❋ The median value of total outstanding debt owed by households rose 9.6% between 1998 and 2001.
- ❋ Bankruptcies set another record in 2003, with 1.6 million personal filings, according to the American Bankruptcy Institute.[1]

"All of that is more than enough evidence to suggest that a large number of people are overdosing on debt," Weston adds.

Today we are expected to use credit cards for everything from renting a car to ordering a piece of merchandise over the phone. Those who balk and say, "No thanks, I'll pay cash" or "I don't use credit cards" or "I'll send a check with my order form" are the exception. In some venues it's difficult if not impossible to make a purchase or acquire services without a credit card. Debit cards, however, work well for many people.

Credit-card abuse is not just a once-in-a-while binge, such as eating too many chocolate pecan truffles or buying three pairs of pantyhose when one would do. It's a disorder as widespread and compulsive as any other addiction, from gambling to adultery. And studies conducted by credit-card companies show how easily the behavior is triggered. A report from Consumer Credit Counseling Service indicates that using credit cards for purchases increases spending by 34 percent.

The False Power of Credit Cards

Companion and Confidante. Women who cling to cards are not necessarily overspenders or compulsive shoppers. For many, it isn't the process of shopping or spending that gives them the rush. It's the card itself. Many credit-card abusers I spoke with said the card seems to take on an identity of its own. It is more than a convenient means of paying for a purchase. It becomes a companion and confidante, much like cigarettes or alcohol to the addicted smoker or drinker. Credit cards appear to provide power and opportunity that many women feel unable to produce on their own.

Escape to the future. Letty said she finds that using credit cards tends to keep her from living in the present. "As soon as I charge a dress or a lunch or an airline ticket, I immediately start thinking about how I'm going to pay for it. I'm just sure things will be better tomorrow, next week, or next month. Maybe I'll get a raise. Or I look ahead to money I'll receive for my birthday or Christmas or the bonus at the end of the year. I tell myself I'll wipe out all my credit-card debt then, and somehow it makes perfect sense to me at the time."

Avoidance of reality. Twenty-three-year-old Kit received her first bank card the same year she went to work as a clerk in a hotel. She didn't make much at first but was promised a promotion and a raise after six months. "That was all the incentive I needed," she said. "I decided to use my card for stuff I clearly couldn't afford, such as clothes and gifts and a weekend vacation. I figured that as long as I was making minimum payments I was fine. It wasn't until one of my friends told me she thought I had a problem with credit cards that I started to think about it. I realized that I had never considered the entire bill my responsibility—just the minimum payments."

Mitzi said she avoided reality in a different way. "I only used my Visa card to shop sales," she said, stressing the past tense. "That was a real trap, though. I'd figure I was saving so much—maybe 20 percent to 50 percent—that I could afford to charge it. But then I saw that I was losing touch with the real cost of the item because I put so much attention on what I was saving. It was really crazy."

Comfort and companionship. Maureen said she feels like a "somebody" with a credit card. "It helps me cope with living alone," said the single,

42-year-old secretary. "My card can always take me somewhere or buy me something when I'm down." Many women agree that they start feeling as though they *deserve* special treatment every time they experience a change in mood or a disappointment. To Maureen the credit card assumes the role of father, mate, or friend who will take care of her. She looks to her credit cards for comfort and companionship instead of seeing them for what they are: a medium of exchange for goods purchased.

When the bill arrives the following month, Maureen, and others like her, are shocked to discover what they owe. One woman said she actually felt betrayed by her MasterCard!

Excitement. For Betty, using a credit card has allowed her to purchase things she could never afford if she had to pay cash. "I like going to the shops along Michigan Avenue," said the Chicago waitress. "I pick out a dress or a pair of shoes and put it on my card like I was somebody. And when the salesgirl sees my card, she asks if she can put me on her mailing list. I like that—being a preferred customer at all those fancy places."

Vera woke up to her credit-card abuse when she reached the limit of both her Visa and Discover cards. "I was mad at them," she said, laughing. "Can you believe it? It was as if those cards were human beings responsible for hurting me. After talking it over with a friend, I understood what I had been doing. I used to go to my dad as a kid whenever I needed money. If he said no, I'd get mad and go to my grandfather or my uncle. I was doing the same thing with my cards. When one would get maxed out, I'd get angry, throw it in a drawer, and go to another one."

Love and approval. Ellen, a 33-year-old widow with two young sons, uses her credit cards when she's feeling sorry for her boys. "They don't have a dad, and I guess I'm trying to take his place by buying them whatever I think they should have—things their dad would have bought, such as a football or a skateboard. I don't want them to forget him, and I guess I think this will help keep his memory alive. But I'm beginning to see it doesn't make sense."

Games People Play with Credit Cards

Credit-card abusers also admit to playing every kind of mind game imaginable in order to avoid their true feelings.

"Gift Certificate" game. Chrissy uses her bank card to charge a gift certificate at a department store. She then chooses an item of lesser value than the certificate, purchases it, and pockets the change. She takes the cash difference to spend elsewhere or to make a payment on her outstanding balance.

Ruth plays a variation of the same game. She charges a gift certificate, uses it to purchase an item, then returns it the next day at a branch store and gets the cash, which she promptly spends on yet another item.

"Shop till you drop" game. Paula says her credit-card spending is equivalent to a marathon. "I go on an all-out shopping spree in Palm Springs, charging as fast as I can walk. By the following morning I'm bored with the whole thing, can't stand what I purchased, feel ashamed, and end up returning the entire batch."

"Peer approval" game. Franny uses her credit cards to keep up appearances. "I charge a couple of things whenever I shop with a friend," she said. "But most of the time I take them back the next day. I just want to be part of the shopping spree. It's too embarrassing to admit I don't even like to shop that much."

"I'll put it on my card" game. This is a familiar game to many women who meet friends for lunch or dinner. Nina, for example, charges the meals on her card and collects cash from each individual. Then she has money to spend on other items.

"Rob Visa to pay MasterCard" game. Marta plays a variation on the old bill paying method of robbing Peter to pay Paul. "I get a cash advance from Visa and use it to make a payment on my MasterCard," she said. "I'm exhausted from all this game-playing, and nobody wins except the bank. I've been doing it for years. When I think of all the energy and time I've wasted chasing money or running from it, I'm absolutely sick. And

yet I can't imagine life without my credit cards. There are so many emergencies I couldn't handle if I weren't able to charge."

Credit-card abuse, like other compulsive behaviors, does not suddenly overtake a person. It results from a unique combination of social influence and family messages and patterns, as Laurel, Joyce, and Becka discovered during their recovery process.

Single and Sophisticated: Laurel's Story

"My dad was a general in the Marine Corps," said Laurel, a tall, striking blonde in her mid-forties, an artist and a researcher for agencies that compile statistics on various social issues. "To my mother and me, he was *god*. He was the source of money and everything else.

"I was an only child, and yet most of my childhood I felt deprived. I remember getting only one dress for an entire school year. My father was very tight with money in most ways, but then he'd spoil me in other ways. We had to ask him—beg him, actually—for everything. Even my best act got me only half of what I needed."

For years, even as an adult, Laurel felt like a little girl whenever she went to her father for financial help. "I had to be practically destitute and emotionally distraught to get a response. It was humiliating. I don't go to him for money anymore."

Laurel's mother didn't dare cross her dad, but Laurel does remember that when he got a little too high-handed her mother would salute him sharply, and that would bring him back to reality.

"One of my earliest memories about my own relationship with money," said Laurel, "is from the time I was around the age of four or five. I had stolen some candy or gum, and I was caught and punished. Apparently I thought that was the only way to get what I wanted.

"It was absurd to even think that I could make money," she said. "My dad was the only one who could earn, and my mother and I knew it."

By the time Laurel reached high school, she returned to stealing to meet her needs. "In fact," she shared, with an embarrassed chuckle, "I stole so many clothes that one year I was voted the best-dressed girl in my class." When I asked her how she handled this with her parents, she said they didn't pay much attention to her, and if her mother did notice an outfit Laurel told her it was borrowed from a friend. Once again, stealing seemed like her only option. "I couldn't earn the money I needed," she said. "Only men could do that."

Laurel admits this belief is still part of her. Even though she had to work following a divorce more than 20 years ago, Laurel still doesn't believe she's capable of earning enough to *really* take care of herself. There is still a part of her that enjoys the role of a needy child. Laurel thinks that sometimes she actually likes to feel pain, to be a martyr, to be helpless. She said that taking responsibility for herself financially is one of the greatest challenges she has faced. Giving up drinking and drugs was easy compared to giving up her financial dependence on credit.

"I've always looked at jobs as an interim activity between my relationships with men. I don't take myself seriously as an earner," she added. Over the years, Laurel has been a waitress, an underwater diver, a private detective, and an insurance investigator. "I went through men like a box of tissues. Falling in love produced a chemical high, much like drugs or alcohol might. It was wonderful. But then I'd wake up, and it'd be over just like that. I went on like this for years because I had no one to talk to, no one to give me a reality check."

Three years ago Laurel let go of her last relationship. She had finally begun to recognize her unhealthy dependence on men and realized she would never grow up as long as she had a man to take care of her. She decided to stay out of relationships for at least a year.

Exit men. Enter credit cards. "That's when I started using credit cards to support myself. I have four cards, and they're all maxed out." Still Laurel's credit rating is very important to her, so she always pays at least the minimum payment on time. She has also figured out ways to get the most mileage from her cards. One way is to charge at the end of the billing period. Then she has a month before the bill comes.

Laurel's biggest problem is under-earning, yet she also sees her credit cards as one of the ways to keep herself stuck in low-paying positions. "They're always there, always available. I can't imagine cutting them up," she said. "I honestly don't think I abuse them. I use them to survive."

In recent months, Laurel has been in treatment for depression, a condition she recognized while working the Debtors Anonymous program. "I think I've been depressed my whole life. But I'm learning now that the problem is inside me. My attitude determines my feelings. I have so much hatred and bitterness. I want to change that." Laurel also wants to find a job she loves and is good at. "It's depressing to do what I hate."

During a break between research assignments last year, Laurel had a couple of months to do whatever she wanted. She gave herself permission to paint. "Something happens at my easel," she said, "that doesn't happen any place else. The act of painting is so much of who I am that it alone is fulfilling." But when she had to go back to work, the old feelings of inadequacy and depression settled in again. "I need a new direction, a new way of thinking. I'm praying for help from God to find my creative side and a way to earn money using my creativity."

Financial Fantasyland: Joyce's Story

Joyce has a secret that is eating her alive emotionally and mentally. She has run up over $10,000 on credit cards in one year and has no way to pay off the debt. She claims she can't tell her husband because he'd be devastated. He leaves the bill-paying to her and takes pride in her ability to keep them out of hot water.

"It's really strange," said Joyce, leaning forward as she talked, her gray-brown eyes intent on the napkin she continually folds and unfolds. "I never spend cash. I'm terrified of it. I can't seem to keep money in my wallet. If I have it, I spend it. A credit card looked like the perfect solution for me. I told myself that each month when the bill came I'd be able to see exactly what I'd bought, and that listing would keep me accountable. But in the past year exactly the opposite has happened. I always need something, and the plastic is—well, it's always there. I'm used to it. I realize now that I've been charging everything from a $3 snack at the deli to a $250 dress at Nordstrom.

"When I get the bill at the end of the month, I'm amazed at what I see. Half the time I don't even remember where I was or how much I spent. I vow I'm going to slow down, but then the pattern starts all over again.

"*Plastic* money seems to be my substance of choice," she continued, laughing nervously. "Not that I'm some kind of addict. But I know it's gotten out of hand. I'm a wreck every morning—scared to leave the house until the mail arrives for fear my mother or my husband will get to it first and see what I've done. I've got to find a way to handle this without telling Tom."

Joyce began using credit cards the year she graduated from college and got her first job and apartment. "The application for my first one appeared in the mailbox one day, unsolicited. I thought to myself, *Wow, here's a bank that trusts me more than my own father does.* I can handle this. At the time my credit limit was only $300, but it seemed like the moon to me. I was making only $18,000 a year at the time.

"It felt like a pass to Disneyland. Suddenly so many of the things I had always wanted and needed were within reach. But at the same time it scared me. It seemed to have a power all its own. I put it in a drawer for a while and kept it there, to be used for special occasions only, such as Christmas gifts or a major car repair. I had always been terrified of debt. My parents filed for bankruptcy when I was in high school, and I remember the shame I felt when I found out."

Joyce looked down for a moment in thought, then continued. "But before long, my needs and wants got all mixed up. I started taking out that card more and more often. Pretty soon I carried it with me every day—in case of emergency, I told myself. But I seemed to create one emergency after another. It was a pass all right—a pass to Financial Fantasyland."

By the end of that year, Joyce was $1,000 in debt. Her credit limit was raised, and again she charged to the limit. "I was frantic. Finally I confided in my mother's sister, an aunt I had been close to throughout my childhood. She was single and frugal, and everyone said she had a pile of money stashed away. I asked her for a loan. She said no to the loan, then wrote me a check for $1,000—'a big birthday present,' she said with a twinkle in her eye. But she made me promise to get rid of my card, and above all not to tell my mother because it would kill her to have a daughter in debt too."

Joyce ran a hand through her hair as if she were reliving the emotions of that day. "I'll never forget the relief I felt. I deposited the money, paid off my card, and cut it in half. I stayed debt free for several months— until the renewal card arrived in the mail. Once again, I put it in my wallet for emergencies. But the cycle started again. Within a year I was in debt again, this time for $3,000.

"I knew I couldn't go to my mother or my aunt. So I got a second job, waitressing banquets on the weekend. I stopped charging and paid off the $3,000 in a year. By that time offers for other cards came in the mail. I said yes to two more.

"But I still didn't see the sick pattern—until I married Tom two years later. He was so impressed with my record-keeping and my eye for a bargain that he put me in charge of our finances right away. For the last three years I've handled everything except our taxes. It's been a nightmare. I put on a good show, but the truth is I'm a kid when it comes to credit."

When Joyce looks back on her childhood, she's reminded of many strange patterns connected with money. "There seemed to be a hush-hush atmosphere around financial affairs. To this day I have no idea what my father earned. I don't remember either my mother or my dad teaching me anything about money. A boyfriend in college showed me how to balance my checkbook. I'm a whiz at that now. In fact, I'm great at record-keeping of all kinds. But I lack financial savvy. I don't have a grasp of the big picture—how to save and invest and when to spend and when not to."

Joyce and her husband rarely discuss money, and they have no long-term financial plan. "He loves the fact that I'm doing something he hates to do. He likes teaching and reading. His material needs are few, and he has only one hobby that requires money and that's fishing."

I noticed Joyce's eyes water as she talked about her feelings. "I'm so ashamed when I think of how I've let him down, and he doesn't even know it yet. It's pointless to blame my parents at this stage of my life. They did the best they could. They were hard-working people, sacrificed a lot for my sister and me, and probably didn't know a whole lot more about money at the time than I do now. It's time for me to grow up, to face Tom, and to get some help. I don't want to live like this anymore."

Credit-Card Cancer: Becka's Story

Forty-eight-year-old Becka is the kind of woman who still turns heads. Her elegant dress, generous smile, and almost regal appearance capture everyone who meets her. But Becka, like thousands of other women in debt, has had a serious and long-term bout with what she calls credit-card cancer.

It started during the mid-eighties when her once-prosperous real estate business began to spiral downward as it did for many agents and brokers throughout California. Becka said she had made more than $100,000 several years in a row during the real estate boom in the 70s, so she did not panic when the market softened. "I had always been a survivor, and I knew I always would be. Several of my friends got out before they lost everything, but I didn't want to throw away a career that had been a good thing for so long. I told myself to sit tight, trust, and hang on."

The first crisis hit when two of her best agents left her office. "My uncertain income plummeted immediately, and yet my overhead remained essentially the same," said Becka, gazing at the Pacific Ocean across the highway from her condominium.

"Times were tough for everyone, but as a broker I really felt it. It was then I started abusing credit cards. I had always used them, but for the most part I paid my bills on time. I didn't have a serious problem with debt for years. But now, instead of cutting back when things were uncertain, I went the other way. I couldn't let myself rest."

Becka said she was determined to turn her business around and to keep up appearances. She refinanced her house, then completely redecorated it and installed a Jacuzzi. "My payments for these loans took half my earnings so I began putting clothes and meals and business expenses on my bank cards. It was nothing for me to rack up $3,000 or $4,000 a month. I kept waiting for the big sale, the windfall that was going to pay all this off. But it didn't come. Instead, I'd sell a condo here and there, lose an escrow, sell another, and then do nothing for a month or two. Then another agent left the office. He couldn't stay in real estate and keep his family going. There I was with space for six agents, yet only two remained, and one worked only part-time.

"One of my best friends in the business advised me to give up my office and go to work for one of the national companies, but I was stubborn. I had worked too hard for what I had. I wasn't about to throw in the towel that easily. I see now that I was in denial, pure and simple. I was unwilling to look at reality. You can't continue to go into debt $2,000 or more a month and expect to survive. But I didn't want to hear that."

What Becka's mind denied, her body absorbed. "I began having headaches and stomach aches, and then I couldn't sleep more than an hour or two at a time," she said. "I was so sick at one point that I collapsed in front of the dairy case at the supermarket. I was rushed to an emergency room and later diagnosed with an ulcer. But even that wasn't enough to get my attention. The doctor gave me a prescription and told me to slow down and watch my diet. Sure. *Easy for him to say. I had a business to run. Just give me the medicine and let me out of here,* I thought to myself."

Becka said she continued on this way for another six months, often working up to 18 hours a day. The worse business got, the more money she spent. She took out ads in the paper advertising her properties, and put the fees on her credit cards. She leased a new car. She bought new furniture for her office, "all in an attempt to prove to myself that I could turn this around. I thought that if I looked prosperous, I'd become prosperous again. I sound like my mother," she said, laughing.

"She was in business for herself too, and I remember she made a point of keeping up appearances. My father died when I was three, and she never remarried. My grandmother came to live with us so Mom could open her own beauty shop. One of her favorite slogans was 'You've got to look the part to get the part.' She believed that with all her heart, and she practiced it too. She bought the best equipment, hired the best help, and leased space in the best part of town."

Becka sipped her iced tea, and then leaned forward and said in a solemn voice, "The difference between my mother and me is that she never went into debt to get what she wanted. My mom also prayed a lot."

But then Becka resented her mother because the beauty shop and church seemed more important to her than her daughter. "I guess that's not fair," said Becka, leaning back in her chair. "When I look back now, she was a young widow with a mother and a young child to support. I'm sure she was scared a lot of the time. She did the very best she could under the circumstances. But for a long time I couldn't set foot in a church. I was mad at God for getting more of my mom's attention than I got."

Becka returned to her story of her descent into debt. "The ulcer didn't get me, but the creditors finally did." Representatives from credit-card companies and banks started calling. Bills piled up. Then an IRS agent called about her unpaid back taxes. "I felt as though I was being sucked into a black hole," she said, wringing her hands absently.

"That was the first time in my life I actually considered suicide. I couldn't see any way out. I had forgotten every positive thing I had ever learned. I couldn't call anyone. I didn't know what it was to have fun.

"And I don't know where I'd be today if God hadn't intervened in a miraculous way," added Becka. "A friend of mine who I hadn't seen in years came down from Los Angeles, and we met for breakfast. I don't know what came over me," said Becka, "but something snapped. When she asked how I was doing, I broke down and told her the whole story.

"She reached across the table and said, 'Becka, I understand more than you might know.' Then she scribbled a phone number on a napkin and passed it across the table. 'Call this number. It's a support group for people in trouble with money.' That was my introduction to Debtors Anonymous, a program that has essentially helped me turn my life around. I'm still in debt, but I did sell my house and am using some of the profits to pay my taxes and some of the credit lines. I turned in my leased car and bought a two-year-old Toyota—just as comfortable for my clients as my former BMW and a lot less expensive.

"I have a long way to go," said Becka, smiling meekly, "but now I'm going in the other direction, away from debt. And for the first time in years, I'm on my knees every morning, thanking God for this second chance."

Taking Inventory

Women who abuse credit cards answer "often" or "very often" to many of these statements:

1. I feel grown-up when I use credit cards.

2. I use credit cards for things I would not purchase with cash.

3. I pay only the minimum balance on my credit cards each month.

4. I use credit cards to charge emergency expenses—sick pets, flat tires, unexpected medical bills—because I don't have an emergency reserve.

5. I am close to or at the limit of all my credit cards.

6. I use one credit line to pay another.

7. I lose track of what I spend when I use credit cards.

8. I cannot imagine life without credit cards.

6
A Dollar and a Dream— Compulsive Gamblers

"It only takes a dollar and a dream." So read the posters and television commercials for the New York state lottery. Similar enticements are on the rise throughout the country as state lotteries and Internet gaming increase.

As the clinical director of Keystone Treatment Center in Canton, South Dakota, Dr. Robert Perkinson treats more than 200 pathological gamblers a year. He is also a nationally certified gambling counselor and the author of *The Gambling Addiction Patient Workbook* (Sage Publications). This book helps gamblers learn the tools necessary to establish and maintain a program of recovery.

According to Dr. Perkinson,

> People who need gambling treatment come into treatment financially and emotionally depleted. Most of them put every penny into their addiction. Gamblers are not bad people. Most of them have never been in trouble before. Treatment is needed to bring the gambling under control. It is difficult for some people to understand problem gambling, but pathological gamblers do not have the choice to gamble, they are addicted."[1]

As recently as 70 years ago it was illegal to gamble anywhere in the United States. Today, however, according to Dr. Perkinson,

Our children are growing up thinking that gambling is as easy as going to McDonald's. Currently, all but three states permit gaming. For the first time in history, gambling is available close to home. People can walk to and from work and gamble. State governments actually encourage their citizens to gamble because it seems like an easy way to collect tax-free money.

Dr. Perkinson said that more men engaged in sports betting but when it comes to video lottery machines, "the rate is 50/50 among men and women. "I treat 100 alcoholics and addicts a day," he added, "and 25 percent of them are pathological gamblers. Women generally gamble to escape pain, whereas men gamble for excitement." Therefore, when treating female gamblers, Dr. Perkinson has a different approach. "We have to help them deal with the pain some other way. We teach them to:

* get honest about their addiction

* go to Gamblers Anonymous meetings and help others there

* get on a spiritual path to God.

Ninety percent of addicts who take these actions stay clean," he said with assurance.

Perkinson also made the point that "many people *know* God's teachings, but they are helpless to live by them because of the addictive nature of gambling. Addiction stands in your way of God," he said resolutely. "Gambling and money become your god. Because of this, gamblers live in hell. Only God can release them from slavery."

The Plain Facts

The National Council on Problem Gambling has developed a Fact Sheet that provides basic information regarding gambling. Some of the facts focusing on problem gambling, include the following:

- Over 70% of U.S. adults report gambling at least once in the past year.

- In a given year, approximately 1% of the U.S. adults (3 million) meet criteria for pathological gambling.

- Another 2 to 3% have less significant, but still serious problems with their gambling and are known as problem gamblers.

- They are much more likely than others to have problems with drinking, drugs and smoking, and to suffer from depression.

- There is also a strong link between suicide and pathological gambling.

- Problem gambling has been called the "hidden addiction," as there are few outward signs until it is too late.

- Some at-risk groups, including gaming employees, youth and seniors, have higher rates of gambling problems than the general population.[2]

An estimated 50 million Americans play poker, according to an article by Mark Sauer of the *San Diego Union-Tribune*.[3] Interest in the game has surged in recent years due to Indian casinos; Las Vegas, Reno, and Atlantic City "pleasure palaces"; "burgeoning Internet gaming sites"; and "television's deceptively simple game called Texas Hold 'Em" which gives viewers an opportunity to play with people around the world.

Help Is Available

Bonnie J. Benzies, Ph.D, a licensed clinical psychologist and addictions specialist, serves on the Board of Directors of the Illinois Council on Problem and Compulsive Gambling. She claims that wounds from the past as well as the present play a significant role in addictive gambling. For example, a woman may have been a victim of physical, emotional, or sexual abuse or she may have repressed anger, guilt, or shame from some other event in childhood. However, current issues also influence a woman's tendency to gamble openly in a gaming casino or secretively over the Internet. She may be depressed over a family conflict or divorce, have legal problems, unemployment, loss of children, feelings of being isolated, fear, or shame. "Understanding these issues will help you know the *why* of your gambling," says Dr. Benzies, "and also ultimately free you from these unseen forces in the future."[4]

She recommends that women who want and need help go into counseling to attend to the deeper issues and also attend regular meetings of Gamblers Anonymous—"the first doorway to recovery"—for the support, fellowship, and tools the program offers.

"For many women," Dr. Benzies adds, "individual counseling may be the first time they experience being the sole focus of a caring adult. It is also a place where they can learn again to trust and be trusted."

Closet Gamblers

Rose, a recovering gambler from Los Angeles, said that in her experience "there are a lot of closet female gamblers." She believes the numbers are hazy because gambling has typically been a man's pursuit. "It's okay for men to go to the track, play poker, or shoot craps, but it's not okay for women," she said, rolling her eyes heavenward. "They should be at home raising the kids."

In truth, problem gambling among women is on the rise, possibly due to the increase of card rooms, Bingo halls, state lotteries, and, more recently, Internet gambling—forms of betting that are particularly attractive to women. Women of today also have more discretionary money to spend, more independence as millions work outside their homes, and more leisure hours than their peers of two or three decades ago.

Dr. Henry Lesieur, a former professor of sociology at St. John's University in New York City, claimed that one in three compulsive gamblers is a woman. Unlike some researchers, he believes that "compulsive gambling is as treatable as alcoholism, yet fewer than one in ten women are in treatment."[5]

According to Lesieur, this is often the case because they do not get the family support they need. Men, for example, are not as likely as women to attend Gam-Anon, the 12-step support program for spouses and families of gamblers. "Gambling has been perceived as a male-dominated activity."

On the other hand, it's unlikely that a support group for families of compulsive shoppers will ever form, he indicated, "because shopping is considered a female activity. In that case it would be the man who would attend such a meeting. But since men, by and large, are not taught to be nurturers, they probably wouldn't organize or attend such a group." This lack of support is one of the major problems female gamblers face. One woman I talked with said her husband confronted her after three years of her gambling and said, "I love you, but I'm not going to live like this anymore. Get help or get out!" End of subject. He did not look for a support system for himself. He did not blame himself for her gambling. He did not try to figure out how to save the relationship.

The reverse, however, is often true when the male in a relationship is the one gambling. The woman will usually accept at least some of the blame for the problem, remain with the abuser, and attend Gam-Anon, Al-Anon, or other support meetings in order to take care of herself and better understand the abuser.

Adventure and Escape

Dr. Lesieur said his research "was prompted by the fact that there was so little being done about women and gambling. Most of the scientific journal research is based on men. Expressions such as 'big shot' and 'ego-oriented' make it clear that the data refers to males. In general, women don't exhibit these traits," he added.

However, as female gamblers have come forward, Lesieur has found "a more complete picture of the gambler, among women, because they are willing to talk about their process. Men don't talk that way." Female gamblers are also "clearly divisible," he said. There is, first of all, what Lesieur calls the *adventure-seeker*. This woman responds to the high-risk action and adventure of gambling, which helps her feel like a different person. "Good girls" see gambling as a chance to be reckless, to go against the tide, to exercise power they were unable to experience during their earlier years.

Second, there is the *escape-seeker,* the woman who gambles to escape boredom, an unhappy home life, chronic pain, or loneliness. Female gamblers differ from males in that they generally do not make their first bet until they are adults.

Members of both groups generally appear to be lonely and troubled women. They also share some common characteristics with women who have other kinds of addictive behavior. Many suffer from depression, a poor self-image, and in some cases came from an unstable family.

Thirty-one of the 50 women Dr. Lesieur interviewed had problems with at least one parent regarding sexual abuse, alcoholism, or mental illness. Many of these women "jumped from a problematic upbringing to a problematic marriage," he said.

Cultural Stereotypes

"Gambling is still very much stigmatized in our society," Lesieur added. "People tend to think in terms of two stereotypes when they think of women and gambling. There is the *irresponsible madonna* who, in the extreme, will leave her infant son in the car while she runs in to play Bingo. And there's the *whore,* a woman who resorts to prostitution when in extreme debt. It's a known fact that a lot of sexual activity goes on in the back rooms of the card parlors in Southern California."

These are the extremes, Lesieur admitted, but nevertheless they are the images people have of women gamblers, similar to the stereotyped image people once had of alcoholics as deadbeats staggering down the middle of the street. The truth is, there are millions of addicts of every kind who live in suburbia and work on Wall Street.

Invisible Addiction

Gambling, unlike alcohol and drug addiction, however, has been something of an outsider in terms of research until a few decades ago. Not until

1980 was compulsive gambling officially recognized as a psychological disorder by those in the mental health field. Dr. Lawrence J. Hatterer, a Manhattan psychiatrist who has researched and written on the topic, calls compulsive gambling "a bit of a step-child in the addiction treatment world."[6]

Even the victims appear to be anything but down-and-out. Many gamblers are high performers who excel in demanding professions such as law, sales, and medicine. Others are successful entrepreneurs, working hard to make the money they need to support their habit. Still others are singles, homemakers, and seniors.

Emerging Moods

The gambling process itself is fascinating. Tomas Martinez, author of *The Gambling Scene,* describes this process in terms of five moods that emerge in individuals as their gambling increases.[7] Many female gamblers can relate to his research.

Risk-taking. In the beginning the person must be willing to take risks. Once involved, she sees the risks as pleasurable. Wanda says she distinctly remembers the day she crossed the line from fear to pleasure. "I put my entire savings—$500—on a hand of blackjack, and I won. I felt so powerful in that moment that nothing and no one could touch me. It was a peak experience. I knew I'd be back."

Awareness of self in the here and now. Gamblers who experience this mood claim there is nothing like it. They are more aware of themselves and their personal power than they've ever been in their lives. They concentrate so totally on the immediate situation that no memory or thought of past or future can intrude. The pattern of betting and mastering the skills of the game builds a person's self-confidence to the point where she is certain she can handle herself in the moment. This mood also pulls her more deeply into the game.

"While I'm betting, I am filled with a sense of living I can't explain," said Betsy. "I know I'm alive. I feel the life pulsing through me. There is nothing like it. Nothing."

Fantasy. The more a woman gambles, the more she leaves "present" time. She becomes free to imagine herself living and participating at a level of life that has not seemed possible before. She begins to believe that she can be whatever she envisions. When she is away from the casino or card parlor, she is reminded of her real life and the problems she faces. A return to gambling appears to be the only escape, so her drive to commit more funds and more time increases. Gambling is no longer a game. It becomes a part of her identity.

Veda said that even after she had gambled away the $10,000 inheritance her grandmother had left her, she was still fantasizing about buying a Mercedes-Benz and going on a cruise to Alaska. "I just *knew* the answer was in the cards," she said. "The cards held the magic I couldn't find anyplace else. I believe it was then that I made a commitment to continue gambling until I acquired the lifestyle I felt I deserved."

Euphoria. This fourth mood, claims Martinez, is rare and short-lived. It occurs after cashing in on a long shot at the races or taking a large pot after a calculated bluff. It is the moment when a woman may feel closest to her real self—the part of her that knows power and poise and presence all at the same time.

Elena recalls a time when she bet on a horse "because I liked his name. I didn't know anything about odds or performance at that time. But I won $2,000, and I remember the sense of euphoria that came over me. Most people would call it beginner's luck, but I didn't. I felt I had a knack for picking winners, and I could hardly wait to place my next bet."

Women who experience euphoria frequently pass from occasional to regular gambling at such times. Preserving their perceived self-image becomes more important than anything else. Dealers, fellow players, and casino pit bosses prey upon such women. They have a vested interest in keeping a female player feeling good about herself while gambling.

Mysticism. As a woman commits more and more time to gambling, her activities surrounding her betting become mystical, almost ritualistic. Dede, for example, said she had a "lucky" blouse that she wore for certain games on certain days. Alice bets specific denominations of money and never varies. Still others perform little rituals such as walking around a casino three times before playing or sitting on a particular stool or in a favorite chair.

Some individuals become very serious about this aspect of their gambling process. They use affirmations, visualizations, willpower, and other mind-control techniques in an effort to "find favor," as one woman put it, "with the gambling gods."

This mood stage, however, can have frightening and far-reaching spiritual consequences for the women involved, including dependence on witchcraft, psychic readings, and other forms of spiritual bondage in an effort to create a lucky streak.

Pathological Gambling

If the gambler chooses to continue the pleasure process, she will stay longer than she planned, become overly tired, and lose all sense of judgment and self-control. Then suddenly she feels the pain of losing more than she expected, is awakened abruptly from her dream state, and must face reality...at least for the moment. She is no longer free to fantasize. She suddenly "wakes up" as she realizes she has no more money to play with, the game is over, the casino is closing, or a friend is dragging her away from the table.

She resolves not to play as long next time or lose as much. But the resolve is short-lived as the hunger to make up for what she lost takes over. The only "cure" for the shifting mood is more gambling. The losses escalate because no system beats the house in the long run. The compulsive gambler continues to use whatever cash, credit card, credit line, or savings are available to acquire the money she needs to keep going. When those supplies run dry she is at a critical point. If she does not get help, she is likely to become frantic and turn to illegal means in a last-ditch effort to recover the losses—embezzling, stealing, writing bad checks, working credit-card schemes, robbing children's college funds, and even prostitution.

At this point, the gambler is close to bottoming out. She can no longer shut out the pain of reality by gambling. In fact, gambling now creates as much or more pain than life itself, as Kitty, Carmen, and Brenda discovered in their terrifying dance with debt through compulsive gambling.

Just One of the Boys: Kitty's Story

Kitty said she's been a gambler since she was a kid. "I was the only seven-year-old girl flipping baseball cards against the garage wall for money," said the mother of two teenagers. "In high school I shot craps with the boys. And by the time I was in my twenties, I was a regular in Vegas. In fact, my husband and I were married in Las Vegas," she said with a note of cynicism in her voice.

"When my son and daughter were little, I'd escape the routine at home by hanging out at the local card parlors. I wasn't working at the time, so I took household money. I started winning, and that made it worse. I couldn't see the sense of paying the phone company or my MasterCard bill when I could use that $100 for poker—especially when I knew I could win."

Kitty said she stayed out all night, left her kids with friends and family, lied, cheated, and did whatever she had to do to keep the high going. "I gambled compulsively for three years," she said. "The funny thing is, I still thought I was a good mother. At least I pretended I was. But the truth is, when I was ready for a game, no one mattered—not my kids, not my husband, no one."

One year, just before Christmas, Kitty said her husband finally drew the line. He confronted her head-on and told her that he and the kids loved her but they weren't going to take it anymore. "He told me about Gamblers Anonymous (GA), and said if I didn't go to a meeting and find out how to get help, I might as well pack up and leave for good.

"But even that didn't stop me," she said. "Can you believe it? I told myself that I'd go to a meeting, lie low for a while, get him off my back, and then be back in the card rooms in a month or so."

But Kitty didn't go back in a month or a year or even 5 years. She's been free of compulsive gambling for nearly 12 years. "I attended my first GA meeting and hated it," she said. "I wasn't ready to change. But I had promised my husband I'd go for a month, so I did. And I kept going back because it started to work.

"In the opening readings of each GA meeting," said Kitty, "newcomers are invited to attend meetings for 90 days, and if they're not making progress after that, they can have their misery back," she said chuckling. Kitty's children were 9 and 13 when she stopped gambling. "It took time, and a lot of patience, but we became a family again," she said with a sigh. "Actually, I was one of the lucky ones. We didn't have to sell our house or go bankrupt. But I did go to work to pay off the $15,000 debt I had run up on credit cards and everywhere else. I owed my brother, my friends, anyone I could suck in."

Kitty talked about her birth family only briefly. "Both my parents were alcoholics," she said. "They died of the disease. To this day, I grieve over the fact that neither of them had the chance at recovery that I've had. I don't know if their patterns set off mine. I really don't know. I'm just going forward now—a day at a time—and thanking God for a second chance. For the first time in my life I know what it's like to be a real winner."

Born to Win: Carmen's Story

Forty-five-year-old Carmen owed more than $40,000 in gambling debts when she went into treatment at the Johns Hopkins University Compulsive Gambling Counseling Center during the early 1980s.

Carmen got her first taste of betting vicariously from her grandfather, who lived with her family while she was growing up. He went to the racetrack every Friday. "It was a ritual," she said. "Sometimes he won. Sometimes he lost. I don't remember anyone making much of it at the time. It was a hobby, like bowling or bridge. But when he did win, he'd share his winnings with my sister and brother and me. He might give us each only a dollar or two, but to me it was play money, money I didn't have to work for."

When Carmen was in college she worked part-time and went to school part-time while still living at home. "I went to the track with my grandfather during that time, mostly because he was too old to drive by then, and he needed someone to stay with him. At first he placed bets for me, but after I turned 18, I began using my own money and making higher and higher bets.

"A month before I graduated from college, my grandfather suddenly passed away. I had no reason to go to the track anymore. But I did. I went for myself."

Before long everything in Carmen's life began to revolve around gambling. "I didn't date. I saw less and less of my girlfriends. I moved around a lot. I avoided my family. I never had a decent job. I waitressed. I drove a cab. I was a window washer for a time—anything to get me from one bet to the next. For a couple of months I was so broke I had to sleep in my car. Yet I still believed it was just a matter of time until I'd win big."

Within two years after her grandfather's death, Carmen had gambled away the $10,000 inheritance he had left her. After running up credit lines, Carmen did whatever she could to shuffle funds. One scam she pulled off with some success was what she calls musical markets. "I'd move from one grocery market to another like a kid playing musical chairs," she said. "I'd pick up a quart of milk or a bag of apples, and pay for it with a worthless check for $10 over the purchase price. I'd pocket the change and run to the next market and do the same thing until I had enough to bet."

Some days Carmen was so overwhelmed from chasing money, she barely had enough energy to get to the track. "At times I didn't know who I was or where I was going. It felt like a drunken stupor. But then I'd see the scoreboard and the odds for the next race, and I'd get into it again. I wouldn't be satisfied until I gambled every penny I had. I figured it wasn't my money anyway, so what difference did it make?"

Carmen looked away for a moment, then continued. "I was a tough cookie in those days. Sometimes I can't believe it was really me. When I think of my sweet grandpa I could cry. He never meant for things to turn out this way. He was just having fun. I made it a way of life."

Carmen remembers with gratitude the first few weeks at the recovery center. "The counselors put all the patients through some 80 hours of group and individual therapy to help us see that we were responsible for the condition we were in and also to see that we had the power to turn it around." Counselors at the center spend the first two weeks breaking through ingrained defenses and modeling effective ways of dealing with others. "I was a loner, and I lied to myself and everyone else," said Carmen. "I didn't want to take responsibility for myself. I wanted someone— anyone—to come along and bail me out. But it doesn't work that way. Women who had rescuers shared in group that the more help they had, the more they gambled. They didn't get well until the pain of pretending was worse than the pain of treatment."

Carmen also made a list of all her gambling debts during the first two weeks—a requirement for all patients. She couldn't imagine how she'd ever pay them off, but she said she felt better seeing them in black and white. "It was a good reality check."

Carmen is out of treatment now and finished with the two years of outpatient visits following her release. She now lives in Los Angeles where she attends regular meetings of Gamblers Anonymous.

She works as a sales rep for a pharmaceutical company, making $38,000 a year. She has paid off two credit lines totaling $20,000 and expects to be totally solvent within the next three to five years, based on a repayment plan she has worked out with her sponsor in GA.

Carmen is also involved in a support group for Christian women led by a counselor in her church. Through these sessions she has learned that people are one of her greatest assets. "I have spent too much of my life running," she said. "Now I have a place to come where I can be heard and understood and loved. And I am beginning to trust God for the first time in my life."

Gambling Away Grief: Brenda's Story

Brenda, unlike Kitty and Carmen, had a protected childhood. "I was an only child," she said, "so I lived in an adult world a lot of the time. My parents were older—they had me in their early forties, after thinking they'd never have a child. When I arrived they devoted themselves to me, took me on fabulous vacations, and spent time on things I was interested in. They even bought me a horse when I was in junior high."

During high school, Brenda's dad died suddenly of a heart attack, and she and her mother bonded even more tightly. "We did everything together," said Brenda. "My mother was a very special person: bright, pretty, full of life. People who knew her tell me I'm like her in all the right ways. I like to think that's true. I loved her very much."

Brenda did not marry. "I didn't choose to remain single. It just worked out that way. I stayed on with my mother, and when she got older, we sold our family home and bought a two-bedroom condo. It was easier for her and for me too, since I owned a small stationery store and had little time to take care of a large house." But a year after they moved, Brenda's mother was killed in an automobile accident, and Brenda's entire life changed in that moment.

"Following her death, I was at a total loss," she said. "The purpose for my life seemed to have died with her. I lost interest in my business, even though I had done extremely well, grossing $350,000 the year before my mother died."

Brenda had other problems adjusting to life on her own. "I realized that first year how much I had depended on my parents for nurturing and companionship," she said. "Usually it's the other way around. The elderly parent depends on the adult child. But my parents and I were like the three musketeers. We did everything together. And when it was just Mom and me, the bond was intensified."

Brenda had few close friends, but one greeting card sales rep she had become friendly with over the course of their business dealings seemed especially sympathetic. "She urged me to get away from the shop, to meet some new people, and to have fun. She invited me to drive to Atlantic City with her for a weekend. She had heard about the casinos and wanted to see what they were like. I was curious, so in a moment of weakness, I said yes, even though I was still grieving the loss of my mother."

Brenda's friend Judy got a roll of quarters and headed for the slot machines. Brenda went to the blackjack table. "I had played the game for fun at the home of friends, so I was less intimidated by this game than the crap table. The machines seemed like a waste of time to me." Before the night was over, Judy agreed. She had lost $20 and decided gambling wasn't for her. "In fact, she didn't want to stay the full weekend," said Brenda, "so we called it quits and came home Saturday afternoon."

But unlike Judy, Brenda thought it was great fun. For the first time in months she had laughed and talked with people, and the dealer smiled and encouraged her. "I felt special," said Brenda, "even though I lost $75. I could afford to lose it, so it didn't upset me. In fact, I chalked it up to entertainment expenses. I'd spend that much on a theater ticket in New York, so I didn't think it was a big deal."

Brenda returned the next weekend and the next. Then before long she couldn't wait for the weekends. She began closing her shop early during the week and going up two or three nights in a row. "At first I pretty much broke even. I didn't worry about being up or down a couple of hundred dollars. It seemed like an inexpensive way to have fun. Besides, I hadn't felt so youthful or so well in years.

"It was another world to me. I'd put on a pretty dress, fix my hair, walk through the casino, and feel like somebody. I could escape the routine of my shop for a few hours and forget my grief.

"I even got attached to a certain seat at a particular table," said Brenda, flashing her deep brown eyes. "It felt like mine. I was sure the dealer had saved it for me till I could come back—which I did, again and again, until I went through the $50,000 my mother left me after she died. But still my shop was thriving. I had hired two girls to take over while I was away, and they did such a good job of running the place I hardly gave it a thought."

Brenda's confidence began to soar and so did her betting. "Gradually I moved my bets from $200 to $500 in a single evening. I could see that my losses had far exceeded my winnings, but I felt certain I'd win it all back next time. Besides, I told myself this was my entertainment. Other people had expensive cars or a boat or skiing equipment. I spent a little on gambling. What was the harm?"

Within six months Brenda was a regular four and five nights a week. The pit bosses and dealers knew her by name. She was offered a line of credit and even qualified for transportation in a chauffeur-driven limousine.

"I was now part of the club—a 'high roller' as they are called. I took out two lines of credit at two different casinos for $50,000 each. But even that wasn't enough. I tapped my savings and began withdrawing money from my business. Eventually, I had to let one of my employees go because I couldn't pay her regularly."

Brenda saw an article about gambling in an issue of *Parade* magazine, and it sent a chill down her spine. "But I was in such denial at that time that I brushed it off, telling myself I was different. I was a social gambler, not a problem gambler."

By the end of the first year Brenda was a wreck. She never got enough sleep, she didn't eat appropriately, and she stopped calling friends. "All I could think of was blackjack. Sometimes I'd wake up in the middle of the night in a cold sweat, wishing the hours away so I could get back to the table and make up for all I'd lost."

The end was in sight...though Brenda didn't yet know it. She went to her bank one morning about two months into her second year, to withdraw funds for the weekend. She was shocked to find out that she was down to $125. "I hadn't looked at my bank statement in months," she said. "I just assumed there'd always be plenty. There always had been. The year before I had a balance of $75,000."

Brenda said she panicked, not because there was so little money, but because it meant she couldn't go to Atlantic City that weekend. She couldn't imagine staying home. She hadn't been alone in her house for more than a couple of hours at a time in over a year.

"It was then that I thought about cashing in one of my retirement accounts. It was all I had left. I told myself it was my only solution. I actually considered starting the process that very afternoon. The only problem was that I wouldn't be able to get the money in my hands for several days, perhaps weeks. Then there was the penalty for early withdrawal, tax consequences, and so on. I didn't mind that so much except for the time it would take. I begrudged anything that took me away from the tables."

Then Brenda remembered two savings bonds her mother had bought for her years ago when she graduated from college. She had completely forgotten about them until that moment. She took them out of her safety deposit box, cashed them in, and drove to the casino that night, arriving about ten o'clock. Within two hours she had parlayed the $5,000 into $20,000. "I was on such a high that I told myself I couldn't possibly quit."

Brenda grabbed a few hours sleep, then returned to the tables first thing Saturday morning. By noon she had lost the $20,000 and an additional $5,000 extended on her credit line at the casino.

"I got into my car that afternoon," she said, "and considered driving off a cliff." The limousine, the free meals, the posh hotel rooms were suddenly history. Brenda was a woman deeply in debt. She owed two casinos $105,000, and she had drained her own savings and business accounts of nearly $200,000. The only thing she had left was her condominium. Her mortgage payment was the one bill she had faithfully paid.

"My shop went bankrupt within two months. I couldn't pay the rent, I had lost my customer base, and my one remaining employee quit. I couldn't pay her. I had never been so low in my life. I considered taking an overdose of sleeping pills, slashing my wrists, anything to end the excruciating pain. And to make matters worse, I kept seeing my mother's face. I couldn't even get out of bed for three days."

On the fourth day, Brenda's friend Judy called and said she had heard Brenda had gone out of business. "Judy had changed companies, so we lost touch for a number of months," said Brenda. "Little wonder! I didn't answer phone calls or letters. I wasn't home long enough to know what was going on. I broke down at the sound of her voice—thinking back to that first fateful weekend when we had driven to Atlantic City together. I told her the whole story. She came over that night and brought some literature she had gotten from a friend who had been in treatment for compulsive gambling. That was the first step of my long road back.

"Like thousands of others, I'm in Gamblers Anonymous now. I'm trying to live one day at a time. But it's hard. I actually miss the good times—or what seemed like good times. But there's no going back. I know that. I also know that if I had continued on, I'd be on the street today—a bag lady.

"I came this close," she said, holding her right forefinger just above her thumb, "to losing my condo—the only security I had left. I'm working at a department store now, and I've made up a repayment plan with the help of someone in GA. I call it my hundred-year plan," she said, laughing, "because it feels like it'll take forever to pay it back. But I can't worry about that now. I have to make the commitment. It's part of the healing process."

Taking Inventory

Women who are compulsive gamblers answer "often" or "very often" to many of these statements:

1. I gamble with money I cannot afford to lose.

2. I am preoccupied with winning and/or recouping my losses.

3. I feel restless when I am not gambling or planning a gambling trip.

4. I find myself increasing my bets in order to experience greater excitement.

5. I gamble to escape my troubled life.

6. I enjoy the status and attention I receive while gambling.

7. I neglect my family, community, social, and recreational activities in favor of gambling.

8. I continue to gamble despite rising debt.

9. I am secretive about my gambling and the money I use for betting.

10. I have borrowed, stolen, or used household or business funds for my gambling.

11. I cannot stop gambling despite repeated efforts to try.

12. I would rather gamble than do anything else.

7
The Great Cover-Up—
Debt Enablers

Many women do not abuse money by spending or charging or shopping or gambling. They got there by covering up for someone else—husband, parent, child, close friend, or associate. Typically, a "debt enabler," like any person who makes excuses for another person, is a woman whose tolerance for emotional and physical pain is inordinately high. She generally suffers from low self-worth and has trouble confronting others.

Debt enabling is a particularly insidious and subtle form of money abuse. Those of us who cover for others are often oblivious to our part in the debting process. We are as quick to rescue as we are to blame, and as eager to deny our part as we are to defend ourselves when pushed too far.

Dianne was a debt enabler. So was Anne Marie, and so was I. I use the past tense because all three of us have stopped this behavior. We have stopped doing for others what they can do for themselves. We have stopped trusting others to make choices for us. And we have stopped the cover-ups, the lying, the controlling, and the enmeshment that made us victims of other people and their debt. But the power to make these changes did not come overnight. Nor did the wisdom or the insight. It was a slow and steady process, and for all three of us it was life-changing. But this experience is not unique to us. It is available to any woman who truly wants to release herself from this self-made prison.

In the following pages, you will read Dianne's story, Anne Marie's story, and finally, my own. Each story is unique to the individual, yet similar in many ways.

A Bear Named Hope: Dianne's Story

"Having money was a high priority in my family when I was growing up," said Dianne, a soft-spoken woman with a kind face and a warm presence. "Although we were always on the verge of spending to the limit, our limit was high. My father was a chief executive with a large steel company, and we enjoyed the benefits of his status. We had a Cadillac and a private plane and plenty of everything."

Dianne's parents also set a high priority on women not working. It was assumed that Dianne and her sister would marry so they would be taken care of. "A nice house, cute kids, and possessions would equal happiness," she added.

Despite the appearances, however, Dianne's family lived with "an elaborate system of cover-ups." Her father was an alcoholic, and her mother covered up for him. When he passed out from drinking, she took him to a hotel, and the personnel there put him to bed until he could return home sober. "I never once saw him drunk," said Dianne. "In fact, I didn't even know my father was an alcoholic until after I was married."

During Dianne's childhood her mother blamed her father's erratic behavior and bad temper on the kids or on his "stressful and important job." They grew up believing their father's high earning power meant that he loved them. Therefore it was their job to keep him from getting upset so he could continue to work and provide for them.

"I was given so much money over the years," said Dianne, "that by the time I went to college, I bought bonds with some of it. I couldn't spend it all. I *always* had an excess."

Dianne married with the same expectation she had grown up with. She believed her husband would take care of her so she wouldn't have to work.

"My husband was a doctor, a graduate of an Ivy League school, and made a lot of money." But he also lied, cheated, had numerous affairs, and threatened suicide throughout our nearly 30 years of married life. I chose someone who turned out to be mean and cruel," Dianne said, pondering her words for a moment.

Over their years together, Dianne did as her mother had done. "Whenever there was a problem, I assumed I was at fault. I told myself that I must have done something wrong to bring on so much trouble. So I did whatever I could to make peace, to keep the facade going." Then Dianne's husband began to tighten his control of their money. He stopped giving her what she needed for the kids' clothing and food and household items. "That's when I started using credit cards," she said, "to keep up appearances. In four years I charged $40,000. One card alone had an $18,000 limit." Dianne paid the bills so her husband was not aware of the mounting debt. "I opened a post office box so the bills wouldn't come to our home address."

But the stress in her home escalated. Her husband was sexually and physically abusive, threatened her life, and more than once tried to strangle her.

"For years I kept my car packed, ready to leave on a moment's notice," she said. "The four kids had their suitcases ready too. They kept them under their beds. The older ones knew that when I gave the signal, they were to pick up the younger ones, grab their suitcases, and meet me in the car."

Despite all this turmoil, Dianne continued to enable her husband's behavior as her mother had done with her father. "I was in total denial," she said. One day when she was out of the house, her husband tried to strangle their middle daughter.

Their oldest daughter, completely shaken by this event, confided in a counselor at her high school. She came home that day and confronted her mother. "She told me there was something very wrong with our family. But I wasn't ready, even then, to accept it. I told her and the counselor that we were fine. We were a normal family, and we didn't need help."

But the kids didn't give up. They heard about Al-Ateen, a 12-step support program for teens with an alcoholic parent, and attended a meeting on their own. Afterward the children confronted their mother about her behavior.

"My son and three daughters cornered me one night in a booth at a restaurant and told me they wanted me to go to an Al-Anon meeting. I broke down and cried, and promised I'd go."

After listening to others share at the meeting, Dianne knew she had a problem. It was that night that she also found out about Debtors Anonymous. "I got into that program right away. I knew I was ready to get well. I cut up my credit cards, made a list of all my debts, and contacted my creditors."

Dianne knew the debts were hers, but she also knew they had come about because of years of enabling her husband to remain in debt to his family. She had lied, kept secrets, and protected their appearance in order to save her family and the lifestyle they had acquired. She also participated in a special meeting of Debtors Anonymous called a Pressure Relief Group (PRG), designed to take the pressure off, as one member shares with two other members her financial debts, goals, and a plan for restitution. A PRG meeting can also be a place to build a realistic spending plan that includes savings as well as debt repayment.

"I learned from the two people who helped me that secrets were my biggest problem," said Dianne. "They encouraged me to tell my husband what I had done, to take responsibility for these debts, and to talk with him about a reasonable budget for our family."

Her next step was a meeting with her husband's psychiatrist. She told him what she wanted to accomplish, and he helped her arrange an intervention—a meeting where she could confront her husband with other people in the room to support her. When they met, she showed her husband her debts and her plan for repaying them by going to work.

"His response was clear and direct," said Dianne. "He said, 'I don't want to be in this marriage.'"

She knew she could not stay in their home with him and risk more violence to the children, so she went to a shelter for battered women until her husband moved out. Since then they have filed for divorce, sold their house, and paid off the debt. Dianne now lives with her grown children in another location. "Even though my world was falling apart, I had to keep trusting that the future would be good because it would be based on honesty."

Today Dianne is working as a nurse and studying for her graduate degree. "It feels great to get a paycheck," she said. "It has changed my life. Now I really feel good about myself." She knows she can take care of herself and her family. "All four of my kids are in private counseling, and we are gradually rebuilding our family of five—no longer six."

Dianne is also aware of God's work in her life in even the simplest of things. For example, one day she bought herself a teddy bear, a treat for the little girl within her. But she couldn't think of a name right away. Then one evening during a prayer meeting at her mother's home, the leader talked about the significance and meaning of names throughout the Bible.

"I still hadn't named my bear," Dianne said, smiling. "So I was interested in what he was saying. That night I had a dream and in it I felt God was encouraging me in my life. He told me the support systems in my life represented *love*, that my job is to have *faith*, and I am to hold on to *hope*. I knew in that moment what I'd name my bear—Hope. Now whenever I look at him or hold him, I am reminded of that message." Since then Dianne has given bears to her mother, her sisters, and each of her children.

The Untouchables: Anne Marie's Story

"My dad was a career officer in the military," said Anne Marie, an attractive 38-year-old therapist with warm eyes and deep dimples. "He liked the stable income and the excitement of being a pilot." Anne Marie is the oldest of five children, and she feels that both her parents set a good example when it came to money. "They always saved for cars, made wise investments, and made money on every house they bought. But for some reason, I didn't pick up their habits."

She does see how she has patterned some of her behavior after her mother. "She was the soother, the more upbeat person in the marriage. My dad was charismatic, but he was also very mercurial. He had a darker side, perhaps as a result of his own father, who committed suicide when my dad was 16. When Dad's dark moods came over him in different ways, I watched my mother enable his feelings. She has largely outgrown that today, but I remember it as a child."

Anne Marie sees that same pattern in her relationship with her husband, Sidney. "That's how we hooked up. I fell in love with someone who is unable to handle money, and for several years I enabled him to stay that way. Money has always been an *untouchable* subject between us.

"I learned that trying to change people definitely doesn't work. So when I married Sidney I didn't even try. At first we had plenty of money. We were both working, and so we pretty much did our own thing.

"For example, I remember a time when we were just getting acquainted. He lost $70 one night playing poker. I think he felt bad about it. So to compensate, the next day he bought me a stuffed animal for $100."

But all that changed when their first child was born. "I couldn't work as much, so naturally our income dropped. We went into debt about $1,000 a month for two years."

Anne Marie was so involved with her therapy practice and her baby daughter that she let Sidney handle their finances. "At first he seemed committed to keeping track of the figures. But over time he got behind and things became vague. To keep up with mounting expenses, he began staggering the payments until we were overwhelmed."

That's when Anne Marie started looking for help. She found out about Debtors Anonymous (DA) and attended her first meeting. After two months, she and her husband scheduled a Pressure Relief Group.

"The man and woman who supported us through the process suggested that we set *emotional* as well as *task* goals," said Anne Marie, "and to this day that has been one of the most effective tools we use."

Anne Marie and Sidney now sit down with each other once or twice a week to deal with money. "Before we get into the money issues, however, first we talk about how we want to *feel* during the meeting." They both said that feeling good about themselves helps them talk about the untouchable subject in a more sane and balanced way.

"For me, having to tell our creditors that they'd have to wait, not being able to pay off everything at once, was the most shameful thing on earth." But doing it was an important step in her recovery.

As a child, Anne Marie had "math phobia," and that left her with the idea that she couldn't deal with financial matters. "But it's not true. I've changed by seeing that I actually know more about money conceptually than Sidney does. I've given up the notion that he understands it just because he's a man and six years older than I am. I've also gotten more forceful." Anne Marie is now teaching her husband what she knows. "I never used to speak up. Now I do, and he's listening. He has been humbled and changed since he started the DA program. He's now willing to keep track of all his expenses, and he no longer uses credit cards."

They are seeing changes for the better in their therapy practice as well. "I'm a lot clearer now about my clients' fees and insurance billing. I'm also seeing that I relate better to couples who have problems with debt. I listen more effectively, and I can help them discover how to talk about the untouchable topics in their relationships."

For Anne Marie and Sidney, Debtors Anonymous has provided the practical tools that have allowed them to turn around their destructive patterns with money. "It's a behavioral experience," she said, "a very nuts-and-bolts approach that works."

She also believes in tackling a problem from more than one angle. "Any two types of therapy are better than one. The more ways you can look at a problem, the more success you'll have at solving it. I like a combination of individual therapy, group therapy when appropriate, and a

12-step program." Anne Marie finds that Debtors Anonymous and other similar programs bring a spiritual dimension to the healing process that is not always available in private therapy.

At this stage of their recovery, Anne Marie and Sidney now have a savings account that is too large to leave in a straight passbook account. By using the tools of Debtors Anonymous they have learned to take care of themselves, even as they take care of their debts. They save 10 percent of their earnings, send 20 percent to their creditors, and live on 70 percent. And at the time we talked, they were in the process of finding investment vehicles for their excess funds and were passing on to their clients and others the hands-on approach they follow in dealing with a subject that was once off-limits.

The Windfall That Never Occurred: My Story

My first husband came from a family with a modest income. There were few luxuries, but their needs were always met. In contrast, I had come from a prosperous home where we had everything we needed and wanted. I never felt financially deprived. I liked nice things, and I was used to them. But because I had not known material lack, I was less driven to accumulate than my husband appeared to be.

Over the years of our marriage, I remember being torn between his desire to acquire and my fear of debt. But I loved him, and I enjoyed the dreams we shared. One day he'd be a famous attorney, and we'd have a wonderful house and new cars. We'd take fabulous vacations—the kind my parents had taken me on when I was a child. I wanted that same life for my children, and I had absolute faith and trust that if anyone could provide these things it would be my husband, whom I adored.

And so we bought our first house before we could comfortably afford the payments. We traded in good cars for new cars. We joined a private tennis-and-swim club when the public court and pool would have been just fine. And we bought our second house, tripling our monthly payments, during a critical time in both our family life and my husband's law practice.

We had barely enough money to squeak through the front door when escrow closed, and we had no cushion for emergencies. I was a wreck on moving day, but at the same time I was in love with my new dream house and with my husband, whom I knew I could count on to pull it off. Every time a scary thought came up, I pushed it away. It was clear to both of us that I was the one with the problem. He wasn't worried. Why should I be? I started giving myself pep talks. I needed more faith. I needed to stand by my husband and support him—keep his spirits up so he could work. But I had a profound sense of despair amid the affluence around me. I felt we were living a lie. Whenever we needed or wanted something, we hopped on the merry-go-round of debt once again, certain that *this* ride would be our last. That "big" legal case was just around the corner. Soon we would be solvent for good.

But the longer we stayed on the whirling carousel, the faster it went, round and round until I had all I could do just to hang on. Something was terribly wrong. I felt it. I knew it. But I was powerless to change it.

Money held us hostage on every front. We thought about it, stewed over it, chased it, spent it before we earned it, borrowed, charged, borrowed, and charged some more. Every time we received a cash gift or a settlement from a legal case, the money was spoken for before we even deposited it. I began to see my life through the eyes of money. Our debts were so far ahead of us that lack continually licked at our heels.

But my husband knew how to soothe me. "It's really better to live on other people's money," he said. "We can have what we want now, while we're young, while I'm building my practice. Then we'll be able to pay it all off with one check."

He was convincing. He was out in the world. He was an attorney. I was a stay-at-home mom. What did I know? My mother had left such matters to my dad. Why couldn't I do the same with my husband? I had to try harder—that was it. Be more patient, believe more fully, and remain loyal. I'd be all right for another six months or a year, and then it would start all over again—the sick feeling in the pit of my stomach, the restless nights, the lack of communication between us, his need to borrow one more time, and my signing yet another loan.

As my husband added to our debt, I attempted to bring some order and control to our home life. I paid all the bills, balanced the checkbook, and carefully planned our expenses for food and clothing and vacations and car maintenance. I loved telling him how prudent and careful I had been, hoping to be acknowledged for my good work, hoping that he'd appreciate my support. He didn't acknowledge me. He didn't even notice me. I had become so dependable that he didn't even have to think about me. I carried the weight of his disorder for him. I suffered the stomach pains, the headaches, the fear, and terror. I was his full-time enabler. I helped him practice his addiction big time.

And he didn't waste a minute. He borrowed, purchased, invested, and spent without consulting me in any way. He bought a private airplane, property in Northern California, part of a ranch in Southern California, and new office decor without so much as a nod in my direction.

When I suggested that we purchase government bonds as a college fund for our three children, he smiled at my naiveté. "By then I'll be able to pay cash for the whole thing," he said with customary confidence. That "big" case would surely come to pass before Julie, our oldest, was ready to enter UCLA—some ten years in the future.

As I write about these events now, over two decades later, I am struck by the level of denial and pain I lived through during those years—pain so deep and so far-reaching that the only way I could survive was to find a way to make his actions acceptable. I did just that. It was my next project. I enabled my husband to keep us on the edge financially because I didn't know how to separate my identity from his.

But coursing through me at a deeper level were the troubled waters of fear, insecurity, and sheer terror of there not being enough. I did not have words for my emotions in those years. I operated on automatic for most of that marriage. It was impossible for me to halt the many loans and debts we continued to acquire. As I watched our credit-card debt reach the limit or another loan come through to pay off the old loans, I trusted, yet again, that all we needed was a little more time for his practice to escalate, for the orthodontia to be paid off, for car payments to cease, for me to find a way to earn.

For a while I tutored students in reading and math after school and during the summer. I saved every penny I earned for vacations and extras, but soon even that was needed to keep us afloat. I became overwhelmed at what little difference it made. I would gather my courage, approach my husband, and tell him of my fear. He would calm me down temporarily with the promise of the "big case that will wipe out everything we owe." How I wanted to believe him!

By the mid-seventies, I was so emotionally ill that I didn't know where to turn. I didn't feel nourished by the church we were attending, so we stopped attending services. I realized I didn't know how to pray, and by then God seemed like a stranger—if indeed he even existed. I was in turmoil 24 hours a day, yet I kept going, sure that things would get better if I just tried a little harder.

I distracted myself by taking a couple of correspondence courses in writing for publication. I loved writing. I believed I had found my niche. Then I noticed my depression begin to lift as I started selling a few articles to local newspapers and small magazines. The first year I made $400, the next year $1,000. Doing something creative for myself helped me regain some sense of self-worth and control. But as I look back now I see that my entire focus was on amassing money.

I became driven to earn. Whenever an opportunity to write came up, I rarely considered anything but the financial end of it. How much could I make to help offset our mounting debt? I had taken on the problem. Now I felt it was my job to figure out a solution.

I see now that I was truly a woman in debt. Even though I was opposed to credit of any kind, I was as much a participant in our debt as an accomplice to murder. I enabled my husband to keep us on the merry-go-round of debt for nearly 20 years. No matter how sick and crazy it made me, no matter how much damage it laid down in the lives of our children, I didn't stop it.

I honestly didn't know how to do it any other way. If I had known differently, I would have done differently. In December 1979, we were divorced. He had met someone two years before whom he claimed loved him exactly the way he was. As far as I can tell, from the minute she walked into his life, he never looked back.

I came out of that marriage with half the assets from our house and half the debts, which were considerable. Still, I had close to $100,000 because he bought out my share of the family house. I was certain it would last me the rest of my life if I invested it wisely. But I was to engage in the dance of debt again—this time with a new partner—the man I am now married to.

Charles and I met within a year after my husband and I filed for divorce. Charles was out of work and in debt when we met and when we married, but I didn't look at that. All I saw was a responsive, caring person who adored me. I had no doubt that he would work hard—as soon as he found the right job—and pay back everyone he owed. At the time I had no idea that I was to become his next creditor.

Once again I took up the familiar role of cheerleader, patient advisor, and long-suffering partner. I had a little more financial savvy this time, but not enough. Even though I was working as a writer and language arts consultant and doing very well, I depended on him emotionally to the point of sickness. In turn, I felt that it was my job to "help" him too, no matter what it cost me. While he recovered from losing a job, I took on extra work. While he worked as a night manager at a gas station and then a clerk at a dry cleaner's and then a stock room supervisor at a cellular phone company, I continued to keep our lifestyle afloat.

We still ate out frequently, went to movies, had theater and concert tickets, and took short vacations—*on me.* The truth is, I didn't want to give up the life I had been leading, and I felt it would be selfish to do these things without him. Meanwhile, we didn't communicate about money except for my periodic crying jags and verbal harangues when I would come apart emotionally.

I continued to write checks each month to supplement his income, to pay unexpected bills as he worked hard to get something going. At first it was just a couple of hundred dollars a month, but then the amount increased. Before long I was writing checks for several thousand dollars a month.

Charles certainly wasn't lazy. I believe he really tried. But like me, his illness around money was rooted deep within his spirit. The natural realm did not hold the answer we were seeking, but we didn't know that then. By the time Charles and I had been married five years, we had gone through my entire savings. At one point we had to reach out to our church to make our rent payments.

The concept of living within one's income or paying cash for a car or gas or clothes or dinner was totally outside my reality. The *idea* of living a solvent life appealed to me, but I couldn't imagine how one could make it happen.

By this time I was nearly insane with fear. There I was at 45 years of age practically broke, married a second time to the first man I had ever connected with in ways that really mattered to me. Yet the same pattern was emerging. Again I was enabling someone who abused money.

One afternoon over lunch I poured out my story to a friend, and she recommended a book, *Women Who Love Too Much* by Robin Norwood. I read it in two sittings. It was as though she had written it just for me. Everything began to make sense. I was a woman who loved too much— a woman addicted to men. When I reached the part of the book that focused on steps for change, I stopped after reading the first one: *Go for help.*[1]

I did. I called a friend who had organized a support group at our church. I attended my first meeting, shaking, crying, and fearful of what lay ahead. Years before I had been in counseling, so I knew that change requires time and hard work. I honestly didn't know if I was up to it.

Once again I felt powerless over my life. I attended meetings regularly. I began reading books, listening to tapes, and attending workshops on prayer and healing. I began to feel different inside, although circumstances on the outside weren't much better. By this time my husband was in real estate, and when that industry began to crumble all around us, we finally hit bottom.

That year he lost $40,000 in real estate commissions from cancelled escrows. The following year, with over $5,000 due in taxes and bills up to our eyebrows, we filed for bankruptcy. It was one of the most humiliating experiences of my life.

It wasn't until much later that I realized how invested I was in money. I had depended on money and men instead of depending on God. What a painful and shame-filled discovery that was.

Over the following months I was led to a support group for people who have problems with money. Did I have problems! I needed every bit of support the group had to offer. I returned week after week. Gradually, as God gave me the eyes to see and the ears to hear, I began to make sense of what had been half a lifetime of nonsense. I began to see that *I* was the problem—not my first husband and not my second one. They had trouble with money, to be sure. But the problems I had regarding their debting had to do with *me*—my self-worth, my fear of being left alone, of being abandoned, of growing up and taking full responsibility for my life financially and in every other way.

Instead I had invested in my husbands, both emotionally and financially, to the extent that I had nothing left for myself, for my business, for my children, for vacations, for my church, for the help I needed.

I backed my second husband's business ventures so he could do for me what I was terrified of doing for myself. I know better now. We both do. We no longer depend on each other for financial provision. We depend on God and each morning, we ask him for guidance in all our affairs.

And one of the most remarkable results of my journey to Christ came from my children. At different times and in their own words each one said, essentially: "Mom, the best gift you've given me, is your healed, authentic self."

Taking Inventory

Women who are debt enablers answer "often" or "very often" to many of these statements:

1. I do for others with money what they can and should do for themselves.

2. I take responsibility for the debts of others—especially family members or other significant people in my life.

3. I assist others financially without considering the consequences to myself.

4. I feel guilty about having money when others don't have enough.

5. I have few or no boundaries around loaning or giving away money.

6. I spend money freely on others while my own needs go unmet.

7. I make excuses for my spouse, adult children, or close friends who do not take financial responsibility for their lives.

8. I compulsively loan or give away money despite repeated attempts to stop.

9. I allow my husband, boyfriend, parents, or adult children to keep me in debt with their irresponsible spending patterns.

10. I co-sign for loans that I am uncomfortable with.

8
Living on the Edge—Under-Earners

Under-earning is a painful and chronic condition for many women in debt. Those who have shared with me say dead-end jobs or jobs with limited potential have left them with a profound sense of anger, shame, even despair of ever turning their lives around. Several said they find themselves settling for or remaining in jobs that are clearly beneath their level of education, below their hopes and desires, and behind other women of similar training and talent because they can't envision anything better. Then, as they continue working for low or minimum wages, they resort to abusing credit when they can't pay their bills.

Under-Earning: A Lifestyle

For many women in debt, under-earning has become a way of life. Some, like Liz, don't fully understand why or how they got into this predicament. "I started working for Arby's when I was in high school, and here I am ten years later in the same place. I'm the location manager now, so that's a step up," she said, laughing with embarrassment. "But still, when I look at the people I graduated with, this is a joke. I mean, come on—still slinging fast food, and I'm nearly 30 years old."

Liz admits that she feels comfortable because she knows she can do the job, management likes her, and it's a familiar environment. "I've received numerous employee awards. Maybe that's what keeps me going." Liz feels that by now she should be in an upper-management position or at least moving in that direction, but the thought of it scares her. "I tell myself I don't need much money. The truth is I have nothing outside my paycheck. I live in a rented room and drive an old car. I have no savings to speak of and about $3,000 in credit-card debt."

Other women who under-earn deliberately chose the jobs they're in because they didn't have higher goals, considered the work temporary, or didn't have a good handle on what they truly needed. "I took a part-time job as a seamstress when my kids were young because I could do some of the work at home," said Raylene. "I had sewn for myself and my kids, so I figured I could do it. Now that I'm divorced, I need more money but I'm too scared. I'm not sure I could do anything else."

She paused for a moment, then added, "When I talk like that I hear my ex-husband telling me I'd never be able to make it without him. I believed him. Apparently I still do. I keep myself in this low-paying job, still dependent on the small alimony check he sends once a month. But that won't be there forever."

Many women who under-earn say they feel guilty when they even consider improving their lot. To some it's equivalent to an act of treason against their families—especially families in which hard work and deprivation were worshiped. Camille's dad taught her that service and hard work were divine and money and status were evil. "How do you go against a code like that?" she asked with a deep sigh. "People who lived in nice homes and earned good salaries were considered uppity in our family. I remember my dad telling my brother over and over not to get too big for his britches.

"Johnny must have taken that in real deep. He's had assembly-line jobs his whole life—over 30 years—even though he had a tremendous talent for inventing things. Our whole family was so full of shame, I was terrified to stand out in a crowd for fear of what my parents would think of me. I don't want to be noticed, and I've made sure of that by the way I dress and the jobs I pick. Most of my adult life I've worked in a kitchen wearing a white uniform and a hair net!"

Meanwhile, Back to the Classroom...

"Women interested in making more money should follow some simple advice—ask for it," says Liza Gutierrez, a writer for *The American Observer*, April 14, 2004.[1] Gutierrez reported the facts on a survey conducted by economics professor Linda Babcock in 2002 that showed "the starting salaries of men who graduated from Carnegie Mellon University with master's degrees were an average of $4,000 higher than the women's salaries. [Babcock] discovered that 57 percent of the male students negotiated for more money. The number of women who negotiated was only 7 percent."[2]

What are some of the barriers that keep women away from the negotiating table? "Women tend to think they will be offered the compensation they deserve. They also believe they do not have much command over issues such as salary, overtime, and other benefits. More men believe the opposite—that they can influence and control their circumstances."[3]

"Babcock and [Sara] Laschever [in their book *Women Don't Ask*] give a hypothetical example of a man and a woman who receive equivalent first-job offers at age 22 for $35,000. The man negotiates an increase of 4.3 percent to $36,505, while the woman negotiates a milder increase of 2.7 percent to $35,945. Although there is only a $560 difference, negotiating the same percentage increase until they reach age 65—4.3 percent for him and 2.7 percent for her—would make her salary almost half of his at retirement. He will be making $213,941 while she earns $110,052."[4]

This is not to say that every woman has to earn money—or even a certain amount of money—in order to feel like a whole person. But many women would benefit in every way by being proactive and accepting more responsibility for their lives—including the financial aspects.

Choosing not to work for a time—while raising children, for example—could be just as responsible a financial decision as going into a high-paying career full-time. Some married couples choose *together* to live a traditional lifestyle while rearing children. It is part of what they see as God's plan for their lives. The wife remains at home, nurturing the children and running the household, and the husband goes to work to provide the income. Husbands and wives need to pray about their unique circumstances, and then discuss, plan, and proceed accordingly rather than *letting* things happen.

Whether a woman is married or single, she needs to take an active, informed role when it comes to finances.

Becoming Proactive

Susan McKean, a certified financial planner in La Jolla, California, and a Christian, says that "acquiring financial knowledge and then positively applying it to one's life is really a way of saying, 'I'm willing to be responsible for my own life.' Maybe no one is ever 100-percent responsible, since there's always at least one little place where we're vulnerable, but we can assume the majority of responsibility."[5]

McKean spoke frankly about her business of helping people with their financial affairs. She too sees a number of women who have never earned, or who do not earn what they need. "They have devoted themselves to raising their families, and they now believe they can't earn very much anyway, so why put forth the effort?"

Perhaps their decision to stay at home was not a conscious choice as part of their overall life plan. Some women, however, did consciously choose to remain at home with their children because it is what they truly wanted to do. Still others may not have had a life plan (I know I didn't), but many of us found the stay-at-home wife/mother experience empowering. Unfortunately, it wasn't conducive to acquiring skills required for work outside the home. Some didn't think ahead to when the children would leave the nest, or they became divorced or widowed at a time when they had no marketable skills. And many planned from the very beginning to remain at home, so outside work skills were simply not considered.

Women caught off-guard at a time of life when earning becomes important may grab the first opportunity that comes their way—and often it is one that does not pay enough to meet their needs. These women need to find out how to establish goals for themselves and then find support for achieving them.

Consumer help groups such as Consumer Credit Counselors and Christian Credit Help provide education as well as practical support to help people manage and pay off their debt in a systematic way. Such help can lead to a whole new way of looking at your ability to earn, spend, save, and invest. Discover how you can make financial choices that are right for you at each season of your life!

"The process of learning is important," says Susan McKean. "As women we need to identify and learn how to state what we want, where we are going, how we wish to get there—and then be able to measure our progress." McKean works with her clients in a practical way. "One of the tools I like to use is the list. I have a woman list her goals on one sheet, then on another, write down her emotional response to each one. For example, if her goal is to buy a new car in six months, she also writes down how she wants to feel about it. Perhaps her goal is to feel good about her ability to research and negotiate an auto loan by herself, or she may admit that she's scared of buying a new car because she realizes it means having to save a certain amount of money each month for that purpose." List-making might also be a catalyst to encourage a woman who has a low-paying job to consider alternative ways to earn additional income.

I remember a time in my own life when my freelance income dropped below my need level for over a year. I became depressed and frustrated. I didn't want to give up my own business to work for someone else, yet I felt powerless to turn my situation around. I met with two friends in a group I attend, and they helped me brainstorm about how I could raise my income. I listed my goals, the ways in which I thought I could earn the additional money, and how and where I could make it happen. During the process, I suddenly realized that I could organize two educational groups for writers in my home and charge a certain amount per month for regular attendance. Within three months I had my program launched. I continued this for two years and added up to $1,000 each month to my income. As I reflect on it now, I'm struck by the fact that this $12,000 yearly sum was beyond my reach until I was willing to look at the possibilities and receive the support and encouragement of trusted friends.

Many women who under-earn find that low-paying jobs actually provide a form of emotional protection they are afraid to give up. If they can avoid looking forward, they don't have to confront the pain of unrealized dreams and unmet expectations. "As long as I'm living on the edge, I don't have the time or energy to look at what I'd really like to do with my life," said Brianna. "I talk a lot about getting a better job," said Wilma, "but I haven't taken one step toward it. I'm not sure I'd know how to start. I don't know the first thing about putting a résumé together or marketing myself. It's overwhelming." Meanwhile, Wilma is a file clerk in an office, earning a little over minimum wage.

A Question of Attitude and Choice

What other cultural influences set up women who already suffer from lack of confidence to remain jobless or to take work that will keep them financially suppressed? Some women deliberately under-earn, clinging to the belief that it is the male's role to provide for them financially, even after a divorce. Others were raised to believe that it was unthinkable for women to work. Therefore, even the thought of looking for or qualifying for a satisfying job that pays adequately can be overwhelming. Some divorce victims want to make life difficult for their ex-husbands or heap guilt on them. They may use under-earning or not working as a way to make the men suffer. "But this attitude hurts a woman," said Susan McKean. "She isn't getting on with her life. Actually it's handicapping *her*, because he usually goes on with his plans no matter what happens."

Spiritual growth is an important aspect of working through financial problems. McKean knows from her own life how frightening it can be to face one's financial obligations alone following a divorce. "I wouldn't be the person I am today without God," she said. "I think sometimes I frustrate him to the nth degree because I have put a lot of stumbling blocks in my own way. But he has taught me when I see a boulder in the road, not to view it as an obstruction, but instead, to climb up on top of it in order to see down the road. And he has *always* been on the other side of that boulder, a very comforting thing to know."

It's very difficult to be a woman today, to be divorced or widowed or single, to develop job skills, to be a mother and a wage-earner. "A positive attitude is something you have to work at consciously, day by day, whether you're successful or not. We all have down times when things don't go our way. It all comes down to how we elect to approach them and the attitude we choose."

A woman who is willing to grow is also usually willing to establish a plan for her life. She looks at long-range and short-range goals. She may choose to remain at home for 10 to 20 years to rear her children and she commits to that plan—but she doesn't let it ground her for life. She views it for what it is—a *portion* of her life—and she may even use some of that time to prepare herself for the years after her children are grown. Such a woman is demonstrating responsibility for her life even though she may not be a full-time wage-earner.

Others choose to work two or three days a week in a profession that does not demand a full-week commitment, allowing the remaining time for family affairs. As I mentioned earlier, when my children were in the primary grades, I worked about ten hours a week in my home as a language arts and math tutor. Another woman did something similar with her talent. She taught needlepoint in her home two mornings a week. Years later, when her children were more independent, she opened her own needlework shop. A friend of mine started a travel agency after her two boys entered high school. Prior to that she remained at home, but she prepared for the future by studying the travel business and getting her license.

Under-earning is not a condition that must be endured or a position in life that a woman has no control over. Feeling good about our ability to earn and manage a salary is as important to our total health as are the physical, spiritual, mental, and emotional aspects. Those of us overwhelmed by fear and a poor self-image can become willing, through prayer and counseling, to embrace the belief that we are worthy of an income that rewards and supports us appropriately.

I hope the following stories of four women who have struggled with under-earning will encourage you as you discover and reach out for what you really want, need, and deserve.

No More Crumbs: Caren's Story

Caren grew up "taking the crumbs." She remembers as a teenager helping out her mother with her own earnings because she never saw her mother pay the bills. "I picked up the slack and took care of my sisters. The problem was, there was nothing left for me. I never learned to take care of myself because no one taught me how."

Today Caren struggles with overeating and low self-worth. As we talked I noticed what a lovely, open face she has and how generous she is. But Caren is just beginning to see the good in herself. "Whenever I applied for a job, I'd set up interviews for the lower-paying work. I have always played down my talents, what I wanted, or what I was earning at a former job." Caren had no education when it came to earning or managing money. "I married at 18, and my husband took over the finances. I had to do whatever he wanted in order to get any money."

Caren admitted that she has been in denial for so long it's frightening. "Until recently I've had no sense of personal responsibility. My parents died young—ages 62 and 64—and I've worried that I might die early like they did. So my attitude has been that it's better to live now and have things now." As a result, she's had a real struggle holding on to money. "The only way I can save is through a payroll deduction," she said, "and even that doesn't guarantee that it will stay in the bank."

After Caren's parents died, she inherited $25,000, which she spent on a variety of things, including a trip to Europe. Once again, she felt the need to spend it, to get rid of it, to keep it away because she was too scared to deal with it.

Caren's ex-husband confirmed her suspicions by telling her when they divorced, "You'll never make it for more than two weeks by yourself." Interestingly, she has made it for nearly a decade, though it has not been easy. She also claims she has proven her ex-husband right by missing credit-card payments, under-earning, and living on the edge.

Caren also has continued her early pattern of giving to everyone but herself, including her creditors. "When I pay a large bill, like Visa, I get a rush from paying it off. I get myself into the mess, and then I feel triumphant when I get myself out." But she doesn't set aside any money for herself, so she gets caught in deprivation, which takes her into depression. However, she's beginning to see some changes. "At one time I couldn't even treat myself to a movie. Now I can do something nice for myself once in a while and not feel guilty about it."

Caren has made tremendous progress in her career path over the last year. For months she had a telephone partner whom she called every day for prayer and support. After months without any work at all, creditors hounding her, and the threat of foreclosure on her two-bedroom condominium, she took a job in telemarketing for little over minimum wage. Then miraculously one of the import-export businesses she had previously contacted hired her as a traffic coordinator in the international shipping department. She has a regular paycheck again, opportunity for advancement, and a sense of well-being about her ability and her worth as an employee.

Caren receives all this good with some caution. "I still sabotage myself in many ways. I spend money on my daughter when she visits, even when I don't have it. I find myself wanting to donate to charities when I barely have the house payment for that month. I find all sorts of reasons for charging one more thing on my Visa card when I'm already thousands of dollars in debt. I play little games with myself, taking from one account to pay another. And when it gets overwhelming, I eat or shop or go on a little trip. I know I'm still confused about my 'reality.' I don't have a good sense of balance yet."

Then, on a more hopeful note and with a warm smile, she added, "But I'm now reaching out for people in Debtors Anonymous. And it's working. I'm beginning to see the power of human compassion to ward off compulsions."

The Root of All Evil: Chris' Story

One of Chris' earliest memories associated with money goes back to her eighth year. "I had a job weeding dandelions from people's yards," she said, "and I was paid by the pailful. I remember cheating by filling the pail with mowed grass and then putting the dandelions on top."

Chris also recalls a time when she stole all the Christmas presents she wanted to give to her family from the five-and-dime store. "I'm not sure why," she said. Then, reflecting for a moment, she added, "The belief in our home was that money is the root of all evil. None of us—three sisters and one brother and I—grew up wanting to make money.

"We watched our dad spend most of his life under-earning. He never did what he really wanted to do, despite the fact that he graduated from Harvard with honors. He worked for a newspaper, but what he really wanted was to be an independent, published novelist."

The family's way of dealing with money made a big impact on Chris' life. "I grew up believing that the only way to get more than the minimum was by chance. There were no savings. We never planned for emergencies or extras. My dad entered contests and sometimes won, but that was the only extra money we had. I also remember that my parents inherited my grandmother's furniture when she died."

Chris financed her own college education. "I paid part of the tuition with money I saved and the rest with student loans and part-time work as a student." She also received a partial scholarship.

"For the last 12 years, I've been an under-earner," said Chris, a warm and friendly woman, now in her late forties. Today only one of her siblings is not in the same predicament.

In both her first and second marriages, the men were willing to go into debt. She went along with them because "I didn't know there was any other way to have what I wanted and needed." She perceived credit cards as her only option. "I charged everything from vacations to family trips, from medical bills to car care."

Chris continued this way until the amount of debt in her second marriage became overwhelming. That is what finally led her into a program for financial recovery. Prior to that time she had begun "thinking about getting more credit in order to have a better lifestyle. It never occurred to me," she said like a child discovering a secret, "that one could actually live one's life without debt. That was a totally novel idea when I first heard it."

She decided to give it a try. At the moment Chris and her husband have about $20,000 of debt, in addition to mortgages on two homes. They are in the process of working out a settlement prior to their divorce.

"I feel a lot of pain when I see how much I have deprived myself by being an under-earner. But I also have a hunch," she added with a smile, "that within the next couple of years I'll be out of that pattern." Chris now works as a word processor, but her training and real love is in the field of social work. She hopes to return to that profession within the next year.

"I now know how to live within my means more than ever before. I keep meeting people who support me in remaining debt-free. I've traded personal items for car repairs. I do volunteer work a couple of hours a month in a food-share program in exchange for groceries at a special discount. I even gave a party and stayed within my spending plan by using paper goods I had on hand and inviting each guest to bring food to share."

Chris is grateful to the principles of the Debtors Anonymous program for helping her discover how to live within her means because it has stimulated her creativity. "I'm now willing to play my violin for pleasure, listen to books on tape as I drive, and take care of my plants—activities I rarely indulged in before.

"I used to believe it was wrong for me to earn more than I needed to subsist, especially when so many people don't even have jobs. But since then I've come to realize that others can't be helped by my earning less. Only *my* circumstances are affected. And I also see that most people are where they are because of what they believe or think. I can be more inspiring to others by taking care of myself first."

Chris was an atheist before she entered her first recovery program (for overeating). Today she has a personal relationship with God. "I see that God has good for me," she said, her eyes glowing softly, "and so I am more conscious of asking for His guidance."

All or Nothing: Miki's Story

Miki, a petite 30-year-old with long, sand-colored hair, is also an under-earner by her own definition. "The binge/splurge cycle and the all-or-nothing mentality run my life," she said. "I'm forever putting out fires, spending what I don't have, breaking my commitments. Then out of resentment I spend more, telling myself I deserve something."

Miki has been an under-earner all her working life. "I believe it revolves around resentment. I left home at age 18 in rebellion against my parents. I didn't have the skills then to live on my own, and I've just never caught up." Miki's mother cautioned her to pay her bills and establish good credit but didn't show her how to do either one. Her dad never pursued his dreams, and as a result, Miki believes "he used his kids as scapegoats. Both my parents blamed us for their problems." Her parents didn't teach her the skills she needed to survive and thrive in the world.

She had a job in an auto-parts store and worked as a waitress. "Most of the time I lied to get jobs. I'd give references of places that had closed down." Miki also admitted to stealing up to $2,000 over an extended period in order to make ends meet. "I had access to petty cash, and I always stole with the intention of paying it back. But then I'd need the money to meet basic expenses, critical things like utilities that were on the verge of being shut off."

At one time she received $3,000 as a gift from her grandmother. "I wanted to use it to buy a house, but I didn't have enough for the down payment, so I frittered it away, writing checks for whatever I wanted until there was nothing left."

Miki was also terrified to ask her husband for money because she was so ashamed of what she had done and because they had never talked about money.

Miki believes that some of her insanity with money has come down the generations. Her dad's father was a wealthy man who was considered a "bootstraps type of guy. He made a lot of money, then lost it. He was also diagnosed as manic depressive and drove himself crazy over not being able to pay his bills." Miki learned that "money was no good," but she also experiences some deep conflicts. "I have a strong drive to have nice things. It takes money to buy them. But I kept myself earning less than I needed and then felt deprived. I'd spend to feel better, get into debt, and the cycle would start all over again."

Today she has a part-time bookkeeping and freelance writing business. "I learned to keep books by working with a friend of the family. Basically, I had an affinity for the work, and the rest I faked," she said with an embarrassed laugh. Now in recovery, Miki reminds herself that she has been sick around money for a long time. "I need to remember that it's going to take more time to get well. I keep telling myself I am *convalescing*. Today I'm willing to do it God's way. I did it my way for 15 years, and it didn't work. A person can white-knuckle it for just so long."

Never Enough: Tammy's Story

Tammy, a bright, animated woman of 35, is an artist and an art consultant. She is doing the work she loves, but she's also an under-earner. Her growing-up years were survival oriented.

"My dad had his own business and always had financial problems. He managed to pay his employees, but there was barely enough for him. There were seven kids in the family, and we pinched pennies for as long as I can remember." Tammy recalls coming home with a list of supplies needed for school, and she couldn't even have a new box of crayons because there wasn't enough money. "There was never any spending money for us kids, so we all worked. Four of the kids had paper routes. I got a job through my sister at Dairy Queen when I was 15, and I continued working from that point on. During college I worked as a waitress and as a clerk in a retail store. I worked twice as hard as a lot of people I knew because I always took low-paying jobs."

Tammy believes her dad's fear of success sabotaged him and the entire family. "He never knew how to handle money," she said. Today Tammy sees how these patterns and beliefs have affected her work as an artist. She does commissioned pieces of art for businesses and individuals. She has done a supergraphic in a men's gym, contemporary abstract pieces for businesses and individuals, and custom jewelry. "I don't ask enough for these jobs. Too often I've worked without being paid." It's customary in Tammy's field to request a deposit before starting a job, but she admits that she is afraid to ask for 50 percent up front.

As a result of not earning enough, Tammy struggles with credit cards. "Now I have only two left and I'm making monthly payments without adding any new debt." At this time Tammy attends recovery group meetings and is learning to take life less seriously. "I can deal with it now. And my self-image is more accurate. Under-earning is such a classic thing for a woman. I would advise any woman to take care of herself and to learn about money so she can earn appropriately and feel good about herself."

Taking inventory

Women who under-earn answer "often" or "very often" to many of these statements:

1. I don't deserve more than minimum wage.

2. I'm afraid I won't be able to make work-related decisions that affect other people.

3. I'm afraid of failure.

4. I'm afraid of what success would entail.

5. I'm not trained or educated enough for the work world.

6. I'm too old to start over.

7. I'm afraid of competition.

8. I'm afraid to make a commitment to a job.

9. I don't want to be noticed.

10. I feel inadequate when applying for a job.

11. I don't know what I really want to do.

12. I want someone else to take care of me.

9
They Can't Say No— Self-Debtors

Some women in debt continually reject or manipulate their environments in order to avoid experiencing the pain of loss and neglect they felt as children. For example, they sabotage themselves by giving away money that is rightfully theirs in order to gain approval. They take on other people's debts so they can "help," when in truth they needed to be needed. They are "fixers," eager to please others regardless of the cost to themselves.

These people are chronic self-debtors—women who owe themselves physically, spiritually, mentally, emotionally, and financially. They can't say no. Although they have many traits in common with other women in debt, they differ in three distinct ways.

Self-Debtors Feel Enormous Guilt

In extreme cases, self-debtors cannot give to themselves at all. These women often end up on the street like Pearl did. She is an intelligent, educated woman, who at one time was homeless. As we talked, she sobbed. Then she slammed her fist on the table. "When am I going to stop this? I feel so guilty if I do one small thing for myself. 1 can't say no to my friends, to my neighbors, to the people I work with, and most of all, to my mother."

Here was a 59-year-old woman still being run by her mother—a frail, white-haired lady of 82. Yet she wielded more power than the board of directors of a Fortune 500 company. She called Pearl every day at work at least three or four times. Her list of needs and emergencies was endless. And her demand for time and service while Pearl was home appeared to be insatiable.

Pearl's mother had always used her poor health as a weapon. "She's been 'dying' for 50 years," Pearl said, between laughing and crying. "Now I'm taking care of her physically and financially. And she never says thank you. She seems to feel it's my duty as her daughter."

The only break Pearl gets is when she does volunteer work at the art museum or babysits during a Sunday service at her church. "The only thing I'm good at is taking care of people."

Pearl is also in financial debt. She spends her money on others—gifts for friends, the children in Sunday school, her mother—while neglecting her own most basic needs. Recently she began attending meetings of Debtors Anonymous (DA) after a co-worker suggested the group as a means of support.

"I even had to think twice about going to DA. I felt as though I ought to be able to handle my own problems. But I just can't anymore," she said as she lowered her head and sobbed again. "I'm out of control."

It was no surprise to find out that Pearl works as a nurse's aide in a hospital. Even her job is an expression of the caretaking role she learned while growing up.

Pearl is a classic self-debtor. Her sense of worth and well-being comes from helping others. Meanwhile, Pearl's physical and emotional health go unattended, and her debts mount because she can't say no to herself or others.

They Reject Attention

Self-debtors usually arrange their lives in a way that keeps love and warmth at a distance so they will not be reminded of the deprivation they experienced as children. They manage or manipulate others in order to keep from having to look at themselves and their need for real intimacy. At the same time they crave attention and are obsessed with the fact that people take them for granted, do not acknowledge them, or never say thank you.

"Self-debt is not as apparent a behavior as compulsive shopping or gambling," said Rusty, a 47-year-old secretary. "You can put your mind around something that specific and go for help."

She shifted in her chair, then spoke again. "I never knew that I was keeping people away by doing things for them. I took pride in putting others first. That's the way I was brought up. Whenever I expressed myself, like saying how I was feeling or asking for something I wanted, my mother and my grandmother would jump all over me. They instilled in me the idea of putting other people ahead of myself. Pretty soon I believed that was right."

I noticed a painful expression in Rusty's eyes as she continued. "When I was in grade school I wanted to be the person who led the flag salute or be the announcer on parent night. But I honestly believed someone else could do it better."

As Rusty got older she avoided competition and confrontation. She was actually afraid to win a game or a trophy or be in the spotlight for any reason. And she was scared of expressing her opinion or her feelings. "At the same time, I was dying to be chosen. I used to dream about getting the best part in a school play or being voted class president." She admits she's the same way today. She's more comfortable behind the scenes than on stage. She'd rather sew costumes for others than wear one herself. She prefers to type a report rather than give one. But she also fantasizes about the day she'll get a community service award or be voted the employee of the month at work.

Rusty wants recognition, but she carefully avoids putting herself in a place where she will be noticed. She has convinced people that she is happy just the way she is. And they don't argue with her. But Rusty is angry with them. She wants them to pay attention to *her* for a change.

They Steal from Themselves

Jolene, a 38-year-old single entrepreneur, has a serious problem but feels powerless over it. "I feel guilty turning down a good cause or a committee that's going to help children, or save pets, or keep a young mother from aborting her baby. I've been blessed, so I feel like the least I can do is give my time and money. I can always make up for it later, when I'm older. Right now it's too hard to say no."

Jolene looked away for a moment, then returned to the conversation. "But I've been saying that for 20 years."

Jolene didn't wake up to her problem of self-debt until she began to feel it financially. Her catering business dipped dramatically because she took so much time off. "I also lost a lot of jobs because I wasn't home to take calls or I didn't return them soon enough to get the orders." For a time Jolene was volunteering 10 to 15 hours a week and squeezing her business into what was left. Not only was she losing necessary income, but her personal life began to suffer as well. "I didn't go to the dentist. I didn't eat properly. I didn't water my plants or clean my apartment or take a walk. Everything I did involved other people."

Many such women gradually learn that their biggest creditor is themselves. "I'm just beginning to see that I owe myself far more than I owe anyone else," said Jolene. "I have not been a good friend to myself."

Marilyn, Jeannie, and Marcie might say the same thing about themselves. Marilyn abandoned herself through overspending and a self-indulgent lifestyle, and now she's in debt. Jeannie's self-debting issues have revolved around her relationships with men and money. And Marcie has expressed her self-debt through caretaking and under-earning. Their stories are next.

The Princess Syndrome: Marilyn's Story

Marilyn, an attractive and energetic schoolteacher in her mid-forties, says she has no money. "I'm like the alcoholic who downs ten drinks but swears she had only two. I'll spend $200 and yet firmly believe I've spent only $50. I have no reality, no awareness of the numbers. I've gone for two months or more without balancing my checkbook."

Marilyn's former husband bailed her out of debt again and again, yet he used money to blackmail her. She often felt helpless in the marriage because their lifestyle was the result of his earning. "I had no money of my own, but at the same time I didn't have to *do* anything. I lived like a princess. We had a live-in maid, a second house, nice cars, membership in a country club."

Marilyn also remained in denial by avoiding any information about their financial affairs. "I didn't want to know anything about money during those years. I signed the tax returns without even looking at them. Money kept me in that marriage.

"I thought it was a good life—parties, friends, plenty of possessions. On one hand I was taken care of, but I hurt myself by staying in a marriage with a mentally ill man who used his wealth to manipulate me. And I stayed because I didn't want to give up our lifestyle." Marilyn didn't believe she could create that kind of a life on her own.

While Marilyn was growing up, her father provided her with lovely things. "Appearances were very important in our family, and love was extremely conditional," she said. "I always looked to outside sources for confirmation that I was all right. To this day, how I look physically is very important to me."

Marilyn's life now seems pretty bleak when compared with earlier years. Her husband lost his business and divorce followed. She married again, but the marriage lasted only 14 months and left her in financial ruin. "I took out a second mortgage on my house to pay off my husband's $48,000 of unsecured debt. I think I felt that if I took care of him financially he'd stay. When I don't feel I'm enough of a person, I try to hold on. But it didn't work."

After a divorce that cost her $7,000 on top of the huge loan, Marilyn hit bottom. "The truth was finally out. No one cared for me. No one ever had. There would be no one to meet my emotional needs."

During the same period, Marilyn's son entered drug rehabilitation and her teen-aged daughter was assaulted and raped. Marilyn put her house on the market, opening and closing escrows on her own.

"Suddenly I went into overload," she said, her voice escalating with emotion. "I thought I would die. I felt totally trapped. I couldn't see any options. I stopped all my responsibilities. For a long time I just lived day to day. Then, for a time, I got involved in a program for overeaters. But what I was really searching for was a program that deals with debt."

Marilyn paused, took a deep breath, and continued. "I was persistent about that and finally I found it. Now after more than a year in Debtors Anonymous, I can say that I am capable of doing something good for myself. I am trying to deal with my pain. Rather than covering it as I did for so many years, I am facing it and looking beneath it. I see now that all my obsessing about money, my checkbook, and my debts was one of my ways of coping. It took the place of facing reality."

Today Marilyn's image of herself is being healed. "God has shown me that he will provide, but I'm still scared to trust. I have a horrible fear that he won't come through the next time, even though that fear is not based on reality or experience. Years ago when I was in my early twenties and coming out of a very bad situation, God gave me a Bible verse that I have clung to: 'My God shall supply all your needs.'"

Marilyn recalls how God made good on that promise when she trusted him for his provision for tuition and board at Western Michigan University. She had applied for an on-campus job as assistant dormitory director but was told that kind of position was not available to first-year students.

Yet that very day a letter arrived confirming a full-tuition scholarship. God had taken her that far. She knew he wouldn't desert her then. Within days of that letter, the Lord delivered another miracle. The position of assistant dorm director opened up unexpectedly, and she was called for an interview. "I got the job," she said excitedly, "and it included even more than I had hoped for—a private suite, meals, free housekeeping, a parking place, my own key to the place, and I had every other weekend off."

Today Marilyn's debt is down to $15,000. She owes $12,000 to credit-card companies, $2,000 to her mother, and $1,000 to her aunt. God appears to be fulfilling his promise to Marilyn once again.

No-Talk Family: Jeannie's Story

"I was the last of my parents' three daughters," said Jeannie, a slim, soft-spoken woman in her early forties. "My mother was 38 and my dad 46 when I was born. I was part of the best years of their lives. When we moved across country from Illinois to California, they built a house for the first time. I remember the love and excitement there. We even had a birthday party for the house.

"I never noticed any financial struggle during that time. My sisters and I could decorate our rooms the way we wanted. I even went to the nursery with my parents and picked out my own chrysanthemum for the yard."

Jeannie's father was the major earner. "He was an electrical engineer and happy in his work. I remember thinking we had the nicest house in the neighborhood, the nicest cars, and my dad had the nicest job. I learned about money from him.

"My mother was a pleasant woman, strong and energetic. When I was ten I thought my mom had a great deal. She could go to the pool with me because she didn't have to work like some of the other women in the neighborhood."

Jeannie's idyllic life continued into junior high, where she was very popular, was involved in various service organizations, and rode horses in the country. "It was the perfect background…until high school. Then everything changed. I had to go to a school where the kids were upper-middle class and more mature than I was. I was not like them."

It was then that Jeannie began to see another side of life—a side she wasn't used to and one she didn't feel comfortable with. "My mother had always made my clothes," said Jeannie. "In fact, it wasn't until tenth grade that I bought my first piece of clothing in a store. It was a marshmallow crepe blouse."

The new blouse gave Jeannie such a sense of prosperity she decided then to build a wardrobe. For a period of time after that she went "back and forth between plenty and lack." These early signs of self-debting may have influenced her patterns with money and self-care later in her life.

Her most turbulent years were between 17 and 24. "I was involved with a man who was really wealthy, but I didn't see how our relationship could last unless I had money too. So we broke up, and I was devastated." In looking back, Jeannie sees how much power she attached to money. Her next move was across the world. She went to Australia for several years and became a successful teacher. That career came to an end, however, when she received word that her mother was seriously ill. Jeannie flew home to see her and stayed on with her father after her mother died.

"It was a very stressful time. He was trying to deal with his loss, and I was trying to help him. Neither one of us had any tools. We had always been a 'no-talk' family, and we still were."

During that time Jeannie met Will, the man she later married. "We lived together for a while, and then for a time I moved back home with Dad. It was a terrible time for me. Both Dad and Will seemed to be fighting over me. And I was so needy I didn't know how to take care of myself."

One of the first things Jeannie did was to become financially enmeshed with Will. "I felt a lot of shame around money issues because I had never had much money of my own. I didn't know how to earn enough to meet my needs, and I didn't know how to manage what I did have."

Will had similar problems. "When we met, we were both in debt and struggling." As Jeannie reflected on those years now, she said on a wistful note, "I wanted him to take care of me financially, and now I realize he may have wanted me to take care of him."

Her biggest fear was that she wouldn't be protected. "We bought a house and started a business together. We used my money to create this enterprise; yet, I couldn't believe I could have it without him. It was crazy.

"I became a cloying, desperate woman. As soon as any feelings of abandonment came up, I wanted to get married. I learned when I met him that he had been struggling with a major addiction, yet I married him anyway. I was so sure I couldn't handle life on my own."

For a while Jeannie and Will lived in Japan, so Will could study art. "Again, I financed the whole thing," she said. "Then when I wanted to go to India to study, I dropped my plans because I didn't believe we had enough money for *me* to do *my* thing."

Jeannie and Will's relationship followed that pattern for years. When it came to her needs, there was never enough, not because Will denied her, but because she denied herself.

The fellowship of Debtors Anonymous (DA) means a lot to Jeannie today. Through its program she has discovered that what appeared to be money issues actually goes much deeper. They have to do with her worth and well-being as a woman. "Recovery is slow-going," said Jeannie with hesitation in her voice. "I have a lot of shame."

She is having success, however, practicing the principles of DA and using the tools of recovery, which include keeping track of her expenses, cutting up her credit cards, attending meetings, and putting a spending plan together. "Actually my problems with money reflect deeper issues that I'm just beginning to look at seriously. Money was a place to start. It helped me get going."

Today Jeannie is sharing her pain with other women in debt. She is talking about it now and expressing her deepest feelings—a healthy sign for someone who came from a "no-talk" family.

Good Little Mommy: Marcie's Story

"I was the second oldest child of seven and the oldest girl," said Marcie. Her no-nonsense manner is a disarming contrast to her inviting smile and fabulous curly hair. Behind the pretty looks, however, is a woman who knows pain, someone who grew up fast and assumed adult responsibilities long before her time.

"My mother was an alcoholic, and my dad a workaholic. He always had two or three jobs going at once. They were divorced when I was 12." That year Marcie's childhood came to an end. "We didn't see much of our dad after that. He rarely called, and he didn't visit us except on our birthdays, when he'd take the birthday person out for dinner.

"Since my dad had had an affair, my mother set out to prove her sexual appeal after they were divorced. She was young—only 33—and she had seven kids. She decided she wanted to have a life. She worked, bowled, partied, and rarely slept at home. I became the surrogate mom, and my younger brother became the surrogate dad. And later he became a heroin addict."

Marcie believes her problems with money started around that time. "My mother would give me $5 a day to feed seven kids. That was my first experience with juggling money—and I still do it to this day." Marcie panhandled as a kid to bring in a few extra dollars. "At the time I didn't even know I was begging."

Marcie has other remembrances of money from her childhood. When she was six or seven, a cousin taught her to take money from her mother's purse. "There was never enough for everyone in the family. The tennis shoes I wanted were too expensive, so I had to do without or settle for a very cheap pair—something I thought most kids didn't have to do. It made me feel less than normal."

When Marcie began dating, she was slow to let go of the reins on money. "I tried to pay for movies and food even if I didn't have to." Later, when she left home and married, she continued her role as caretaker and the self-debt increased. "I was the top student in trade school. I got a full-time job because I knew I'd need it—even though at the time I married it was the norm for the husband to work full-time and the wife part-time or not at all.

"My mother's message to me was 'Don't ever expect money from men.'" So Marcie didn't. "I took control. I didn't want the men in my life to work, or they might leave me." Her first husband obliged, whether he realized it or not. He had 15 jobs in 12 years.

Marcie's dad also used money to control his children as adults. For example, "One year he wanted to buy me furniture as a house-warming present. He bought a couch, love seat, two chairs, and a coffee table at an estate sale. He was trying to please me," she said, smiling, "but he obviously didn't know me. His choices were dark, depressing antiques. I wanted floral prints," she said, her tone lightening as she spoke, "to reflect my recovering self."

Her dad was relating to Marcie's old self. "He only knew what he had created—someone who would please him and be forever grateful. His message was 'Don't be who you are, be who I want you to be.' He always called me 'a good little mommy.'"

"My dad was a 'coupon person.' He never bought anything unless it was a good deal. I remember him driving 100 miles once to bring me a coupon."

Marcie sees herself repeating the family pattern today. She was divorced after 11 years of marriage, just like her mother and father. The one difference, however, is that she and her two children are in recovery. Still, breaking old patterns does not come easy. "I hurt myself by bingeing and purging with money. I'm trying to identify what I do and why I let my bills go for two months at a time."

Marcie is also trying for the first time to learn about nutrition. "I was never taught how to cook or eat properly. I know we eat out too much. Maybe I'm making up for the past when I had to do all the cooking." Housekeeping and bill-paying also stir up painful memories. "When money is tight, it brings up thoughts that there won't be enough. I remember as a kid that by the time I got to the table after cooking for my brothers and sisters there was no food left for me."

Marcie also sabotaged herself by using food to help her deal with grief. When she learned that her brother had committed suicide, she handled the overwhelming feelings by eating.

She was also the "family hero." Once she gave $1,000 to a woman who needed it—even though Marcie needed it just as much or more. She is also an incest survivor and a workaholic. "I qualify for every self-help program ever created," she said in a burst of laughter.

"I never planned anything. Life just happened to me. I have to trick myself in order to plan. I need to make myself face my 'busy' addiction, which I use to avoid doing what I *really* want to do. I want to play the piano," she said wistfully, "but I sold my piano for $50 because I needed the money." Marcie, like so many other self-debtors, has a hard time giving herself the things that really matter because she keeps busy deflecting the pain of the past and its healing truth.

But Marcie is not willing to stay in pain and denial. She's in therapy now and attends several support groups. And she says she wants to build a relationship with God. "But the idea of a power greater than me is a difficult one because for so long I was 'it'—the only one I could count on."

Today Marcie is taking what she calls baby steps. "I need to change jobs, but I feel paralyzed. I bought a Sunday paper so I could read the want ads. I haven't opened it yet, but at least I bought it. That's a start."

Facing the Pain

To break the chain of self-debting behavior we have to move toward the truth about the past, the truth about our parents. Eventually we have to accept what we discover. But this is a process that requires time, patience, and prayer...and sometimes the help of a professional coach or counselor.

Some of us hurt because we were hurt. Our parents didn't know how to listen to our feelings without feeling hurt themselves. Probably they didn't receive all that they needed from their mothers and fathers. It helps to acknowledge this so we don't continue to blame them. Many simply didn't know any more than we do.

Pain is a sign that something is wrong and needs correction. If we walk toward it we can overcome it. If we avoid it, it follows us wherever we go. God did not intend for us to walk this path alone, however. Professional and spiritual help are available to anyone who reaches for them. There are licensed therapists who specialize in victimization and depression— common symptoms of self-debting. You can find names and phone numbers for these professionals through a church, a community mental health service, the Internet, or as a referral from someone you trust.

Taking Inventory

Women who are self-debtors answer "often" or "very often" to these statements:

1. I always think of others before I think of myself.

2. I can't say no.

3. I crave attention, though I hide from it.

4. I focus on others so I won't have to look at myself.

5. I am quick to discount my own needs in order to gain acceptance.

6. I cannot give to myself without feeling guilty.

7. I have trouble making decisions that involve my life.

8. I spend money on others at the expense of my own needs.

10

Barefoot and Broke— Perpetual Paupers

At the opposite end of the debt spectrum are perpetual paupers—women who are compelled to push away whatever money they have. These individuals *must* get rid of their money as fast as it comes in. They are not necessarily overspenders, although they might be, and they do not necessarily use credit cards. They might not owe anyone anything. Spending money on themselves may not be a problem for them the way it is for self-debtors. They might not gamble, shop, spend in excess, or under-earn, but nonetheless they, too, are crazy around money. Paupers cannot keep money. They cannot save it, invest it, or hold on to it in any form. They are compelled to live on the edge.

The women I spoke with who identify with this behavior said it is as baffling to them as it is to those around them. Many make enough money to meet their needs and wants, but they get rid of it as fast as they earn it with no thought of what is really important to them. Some are under-earners, also an expression of their compulsion to keep money at a distance. And still others are flat broke all the time, working intermittently, squandering or giving away what does come in, and generally living a hand-to-mouth existence even though a better life is possible. Several traits seem to characterize the perpetual pauper.

An Obsession with Acquiring Money

Amy, a 31-year-old elementary schoolteacher, has a perfectly adequate salary and benefits, yet she has an exaggerated fear of economic insecurity. "I'm always looking for ways to get more money," she said. "I tutor reading students a couple of evenings a week. I teach English to a foreign student. I find myself planning ahead for money I know I'll receive for my birthday or Christmas. But no matter how much I have, it's never enough."

Simone can relate to this same compulsion. She donates blood to earn extra money when she's in need, and she and a friend take things to sell at a flea market in their city. "I heard a lot of contradictory messages at home," said the smiling, soft-spoken 30-year-old dressed in tattered blue jeans and T-shirt. "My mom handled the money in our family, and the message was 'We don't have enough.' But every year before school started it was better than Christmas. We got everything we needed and wanted." Simone believes "money covered the guilt my parents felt at not having a personal relationship with their kids. It was their currency of love."

An Obsession with Getting Rid of Cash

At the same time that Amy and Simone are looking for ways to get more money, they also admit to their need to get rid of it by spending it or giving it away as fast as it comes in. "I'm a sucker for every charity that approaches me by phone or mail," said Amy. "I can't go to the grocery store without stocking up for months. There's a part of me that hoards stuff. I have enough toilet paper for a year, canned goods for months ahead of time—when the money could have been used to pay bills or to save for something really nice for myself. I'm always on the edge financially, struggling the last few days each month till payday."

Amy looks at other teachers she knows, and they seem to be fine. They have decent clothes and adequate cars, and they take good vacations during their time off. "I *want* this for myself," she said, "but I have a hard time making it happen. One year I actually saved $200 in a special vacation account, but I felt restless every time the bank statement arrived. I felt like I should use it for something important."

She got her chance in December of that year when the brakes on her car went out and she had to spend her vacation fund on repairs. "I actually felt relieved to be drawing out that money. It always seemed wrong to have it just sitting there."

Simone remembers her first experience of "blowing all the money I had." She had saved $100 and "felt nervous and excited about spending it. I spent it all. My mother was so disappointed in me. She wanted me to save it for a rainy day." As an adult, the cycle continued. "Until I got help, I had almost no awareness of how to handle money. I had a hard time seeing that I had choices."

Simone has a pauper compulsion. "I have to get rid of my money to make room for more. I feel that if I spend it, then I can have more." But as soon as more comes in, she spends that too, and the pattern repeats itself. And her mother has fed her disease. "She'd send money. I'd spend it. She'd get upset and then send me more. One time it would be $700; another time it would be $8,000."

Today Simone does not ask her parents for money for any reason. "I want to break the cycle. I want to be responsible for myself."

An Obsession with Lying to Oneself

Amy has abandoned her hopes and dreams for her life. "I live in an apartment even though I could own a condominium. I started out with only a cot and a table and chair, and that was it for the longest time. I never entertained because I didn't want anyone to see the way I lived," she said, with a hint of shame in her voice. "The only reason I have any furniture now is because my aunt died and my mother offered me her things. They're not my taste, but I don't have money to get what I really want—at least not right now."

Amy also fears she could become self-indulgent if she had enough money to do what she'd like. "It's probably better that I don't have a surplus. I couldn't trust myself to spend it prudently." Realistically Amy could save enough money to buy the possessions she yearns for. But she fears success so she lies to herself by saying she doesn't have enough money to get what she needs and wants.

Simone, too, admits that her pauper mentality has kept her from her true self, from doing what she really wants to do, which is to play the piano and go to graduate school for a science degree. She'd like money for a piano and lessons and for tuition and books. And she'd really like to take a vacation—for the first time in many years. Even as she reviews her desires, Simone admits that when it comes to money, "I'm afraid of blowing it all. But then I think of what I want, and the conflict starts again. My wants always exceed the money I have."

For Simone this is an old pattern. She voices her dreams and wishes and then lies to herself about there not being enough money to make them happen. "I remember as a kid getting money and making a list of what I wanted. I'd feel frightened and excited at the same time. It was the kind of emotional rush you feel when you're in love. I remember a pair of sunglasses I bought and then lost before I fell out of love with them. It was awful."

Today Simone attends Debtors Anonymous meetings, and she works with a life coach. "The personal contact with other people in the program and sharing my own struggles are the strong ties that are helping me become more responsible with the money I have."

Perpetual paupers—contrary to the stereotypical image of a bag lady pushing a grocery cart stuffed with junk—are women like you and me. They are found in every walk of life and are of every background and belief. The *pauper compulsion* is, first of all, a state of mind fueled by a set of beliefs that drive the unwanted behavior.

Kelly, Nancy, and July know about the pauper mentality firsthand. They've agreed to share their stories.

Hand-to-Mouth: Kelly's Story

"I used to think pauperism was the same as self-debting," said Kelly, a 33-year-old administrative assistant. "But actually it's not. Self-debting means I can't give to myself even though I may have the money to do so. Being a pauper means I *have to get rid* of my money."

At the same time, she *wants* money all the time. "I'm always scheming to get it. I take part-time jobs. And I sell things and wonder how much I'll make. Yet my husband and I make enough to live on."

While Kelly was growing up, there was never enough food or money. Her whole childhood was hand-to-mouth. "There was *never* an excess," she said, stressing the negative. "When I was about five, my mother became a single parent. I remember emptying my piggy bank for her." Even the *subject* of money has a shaming effect on Kelly. "Whether I have it or I don't have it, I feel shame," she said. Today it is very hard for her to distinguish between wants and needs. "For so long our family never had enough to pay bills. Now I *have* to pay and spend until there's nothing left."

She can't buy groceries for just a week. She buys enough for a month. "If I have money, I feel compelled to get rid of it, even if the purchases don't make sense. I also sabotage myself by spending the money that should be used for bills." At one point Kelly actually accumulated $500 in savings, but she couldn't leave it there. "I spent it all on gas, electricity, and phone bills. I took away from myself in order to pay bills."

Kelly's husband has what she calls "complementary addictions." He is an overspender and a self-debtor. "I spend like mad, and he buys *me* things, but he can't spend money on himself. He seems to need my permission. For example, he might run out of shaving cream. He'll keep talking about needing it, but won't actually go to the store and buy it."

Kelly, her dark eyes intent as she spoke, said she is now learning a lot about money and compulsive behavior. "It's taken me four years to understand addiction. I'm learning to take things back to the store, though it's embarrassing. I'm also putting away some money just for me, and it feels good. I have $500 surplus in a checking account now, and it's going to stay there."

Kelly's recovery started in Narcotics Anonymous (NA) and is now continuing in Debtors Anonymous. "I found God in NA," she said with a lilt in her voice. "My spiritual life is now the most important thing in my life." But spirituality wasn't important in her family while she was growing up. Her family had what she called a religion-of-the-month. "Guilt, punishment, and perfectionism were the grounds. I was already shamed at home, so this didn't help." But when she had a spiritual awakening in NA, she aligned her will with God's. "I can remember honestly hearing him telling me gently that there is abundance for me. Today I really *have* it."

Thread of Love: Nancy's Story

Nancy was born in Sioux Falls, South Dakota, and was adopted as an infant. She remembers two beliefs that guided her early life and influenced her as an adult. "First, I learned that I couldn't count on people—even my parents. I had to take care of myself. Once I learned that, I threw people out of my life. Second, I learned at church and in parochial school that the only perfect family was the Holy Family. So when I realized my family couldn't be perfect, I threw God out of my life too."

While growing up Nancy also received a continuous message that "you can't have what you want." "Like my mother, I was second best, and I always got second best. I hid out in school and did very well, but my mother always put down my grades. I remember buying candy to make myself feel better."

Nancy's spending and shopping began when she was about 15. "My mother was working then, so my refuges were the library, where it was quiet and orderly, and Fantal's Department Store because of its beautiful things. I believe I felt more like God's child in Fantal's than anywhere else. I felt prosperous when I was there. The bright, beautiful colors and shapes brought out my creativity."

But like most paupers, Nancy was influenced by her family patterns. She liked beautiful things, but she wasn't able to have them, so again she made school her haven and attained bachelor's, master's, and doctoral degrees. Then, just like her mother, she went to work as a paralegal.

She married her first and only husband for the $10,000 he had at the time. She wanted him to take care of her, but it wasn't a marriage of love, and shortly afterward she began drinking. "In December of 1974, one day I woke up on the living room floor, drunk. I was 34 years old at the time. My father had died of alcoholism at the same age. Suddenly I saw how I was repeating the pattern. Right then I stopped—and went to my first Alcoholics Anonymous meeting."

That same year, Nancy became restless for the truth about her birth parents, and she traced her mother to Minnesota. She learned that both her birth mother and her adoptive mother had worked for the same attorney. "All my abandonment issues came up the day I went to meet my natural mother. We looked just alike. I knew I was her daughter." They kept in contact for a while, but in recent years they have not seen each other.

In the mid-seventies, Nancy and her husband moved to California. At the time they had $120,000 between them. By the end of the decade they were divorced, and Nancy had $34,000 to start a new life. For a time she "pretended to be a realtor," but that wasn't for her. She moved and went into workaholism: "I became cold and hard. By the time I hit Debtors Anonymous in August 1990, I had no heart and no soul left."

After attending a few Debtors Anonymous meetings, she swung the other way, stopped spending altogether, and went into what she calls her miser phase. "I learned how to put a spending plan together, but after a few months, I stopped going to meetings." She said she got what she needed and knew it was time to move on.

Today God has a place in Nancy's life—for the first time ever—and she said she feels His presence. "Now I take God into my work. I am more trusting, more sharing, and more approachable than ever before. My creative energy has soared. I see colors again, and I feel my emotions. I'm more myself and less an actor."

Now Nancy knows that God will provide. She no longer has to rid herself of money and possessions in order to repeat the past. "I believe God is leading me into my creativity more and more. I'm trusting him to meet my needs, and I'm taking small typing jobs as they come along, until I know what I'm supposed to do next. I'm an artist at heart. Right now I know I'd like to work in an art museum, and I want to train to become a docent."

And what about clothing for the new Nancy, who once longed to dress like the mannequins at Fantal's? "I buy my clothes at the Bargain Bungalow," she said, with a confident smile. "It's a resale shop a couple of blocks from where I live, and it has all the fashions I like at the prices I can afford."

As for her career in the legal field, it's a thing of the past along with drinking and binge-spending and a marriage that was never meant to be. "I withdrew from law because when I work there I lose the thread of love in my life," the thread that carried Nancy from Minnesota to California and lifted her from pauperism to prosperity of the spirit.

Mixed Messages: July's Story

"My dad was a colonel in the Air Force," said July, an athletic woman with a warm smile and rapid-fire speech that demands you pay attention. I was drawn in by her enthusiasm and attentiveness.

"To us, his rank meant that we were better than others," she said. But at the same time, both her mother and father were practicing alcoholics. So the parental messages were mixed right from the start.

"I have an incredible history," said July, as she ran down the list of luxuries that permeated her early years. "For a time we lived in France in a chateau on 26 acres. The house had 13 bedrooms and 4 bathrooms," she exclaimed, seemingly impressed all over again as she shared the story of her unusual upbringing.

The association with money and power was laid down early in July's life. "I remember a time when I was about seven or eight. I saw my folks in a fight with the landlord. I thought to myself, *We have money; this can't happen to us.*" The confusing dynamics in her parents' relationship with each other also caused her to receive mixed messages about money.

"Dad said we had enough. Mom said we didn't. It wasn't until three months ago that I learned the truth. They have close to a million dollars in assets—money that I'll come into one day. But when I think about it, it's really hard for me to believe that for myself."

July has always pictured herself as not being capable, even though her parents never actually said anything negative to her. However, her father did most things involving money for her. "I took my checkbook to my dad for balancing. And when I was old enough to drive, he bought me a car. But I couldn't handle it by myself. When I got a flat tire I gave the car back to him. My folks also bought me a house." But that too became an overwhelming responsibility. "I remember being terrified to spend and to make decisions about money. I put only $37 on my credit card in two years. I was afraid of it!"

As a young adult, July gradually buried her insecurities in drugs and alcohol until those too overwhelmed her, and she turned to Alcoholics Anonymous for help. "But as soon as I got sober, my money addiction surfaced. I started ridding myself of all my money. I maxed out my credit cards. I bought things I didn't need or want. I couldn't keep up my house. I finally sold it to pay my debts, even though the message from home had been 'Don't sell property.'"

Even those experiences were not enough to stop her from pushing away the money she had through wild spending and charging. "I went right back into debt, this time up to 7,000 or 8,000 dollars."

By then July knew her way around support programs, and she began attending meetings of Debtors Anonymous. She also met the man in her life about that same time and discovered that he has the same fear she has—the fear of not having enough. "We are both paupers. We have very mushy boundaries when it comes to money," she added.

July has "a real struggle" keeping more than $500 in savings at one time. "When it gets to that amount, something always happens. I notice that it's almost a relief when I get the balance below $500 again." July also pushes money away by buying stuff that doesn't mean anything. "I have nothing to show for all the money I've spent."

However, she has made one significant personal commitment: She's returned to sports. "I'm now involved in triathalon competitions: swimming, biking, and running. And this requires spending some money. There's a hefty entry fee that I'm now willing to pay, and I've also invested in an expensive camera for my career."

July took a moment to talk about her spiritual life. She said that when she entered her first recovery program she had "a spurt of enormous spiritual growth, but then it slowed down. I think I was afraid of becoming a self-help junkie," she said, laughing. "But now I'm beginning to feel spiritually flabby. I'm losing my tone. I know what it's like to surrender. I know there's a greater power than me. However, at this point in my life, I don't understand it. But I do respect it."

Taking Inventory

Women who are perpetual paupers answer "often" or "very often" to many of these statements.

1. I push money away.

2. I feel relieved when I have to spend money.

3. I have a difficult time keeping money in a savings account.

4. I keep myself on the edge financially.

5. I'm scared that I won't be able to handle money responsibly.

6. I am uncomfortable with large sums of money.

7. I find a way to spend or give away my money.

8. I spend money set aside for bills on items I don't need or want.

Part 3
Ending the
Madness

11
Telling and Receiving the Truth

In 1978, I made an appointment with a counselor I had met some years before while doing research for one of my books. I had been impressed by his compassion, his professionalism, and, most important to me at the time, his empathy for troubled marriages.

I remember sitting in his office waiting room the afternoon of my first session, leafing through a magazine as my right leg bounced nervously atop my left knee. "Get in, get a few tips, and get out," I told myself. I had no intention of entering long-term counseling. I honestly believed the solution to my problems could be contained on a recipe card. Wisely, the counselor encouraged me to share my story. After I rushed through the chronology of events and behaviors, I sat back in my chair and waited for him to tell me what to *do*.

"How do you feel about all this?" he asked, giving special emphasis to the word *feel*.

"Feel? What do you mean how do I feel?" I asked, repeating his question with a touch of annoyance.

"I'm wondering what it feels like," he persisted, "to be treated in such an uncaring way, to be in debt, to be neglected, to be set aside for another woman."

"I don't know," I said, dumbfounded. "Is it important to know how I feel? No one's ever asked me how I felt about anything in my whole life. I've just tried to do what's right. I hoped you'd tell me the right thing to do now."

The Truth About Me

I'll never forget that experience. It was the day I became acquainted with my emotional self. I needed some help putting my feelings into words, but before I left the counseling office, I was able to say that I felt *hurt, sad,* and *disappointed.* It was a start. Admitting those feelings led to uncovering deeper levels of emotion, and over time I was finally able to express the most frightening feelings of all—guilt, anger, and finally rage.

I'm sharing this because it demonstrates in a very personal way the power of telling the truth as we *experience* it—not simply as we know it. I knew a *lot* of information. I had even written articles about women and money and about communication in marriage. But they were of little benefit to me during my crisis because I was hurting so much.

That first session of private therapy opened a door within that had been closed and locked most of my life. The sad part is, I didn't even know there was anything under lock and key. I had lived my life as a *doer.*

During the months in counseling, however, I began to see tiny glimpses of a side of life I had never known. I began to *feel.* Pain. Sadness. Anger. I was coming alive. Choices and options seemed available for the first time. It was okay for me to tell my husband no, that I would not co-sign for another loan. It was all right to say I felt angry and hurt when he walked out on a conversation with me.

I also noticed that whenever I was able to express my emotions honestly, I would feel better inside immediately. Gradually I felt a change in my physical health as well. I had fewer headaches, stomach cramps, and colon spasms and less upper back pain. And the more I voiced my feelings, the less power my negative thoughts had. I became more playful, more responsive, more available to people and to life.

This process of self-discovery reminded me of a time I took my sewing machine apart and put it back together again. I had gone after a thread that was jamming the system. I uncovered one part at a time and set it aside in an orderly way until I got to the thread. Then I plucked it out, tossed it away, and slowly and carefully put the pieces back together. Finally I turned on the machine and sewed a few test stitches. It worked! In a similar way, I had begun taking myself apart, going after the thread of truth that I knew was caught on some interior part of me. As I slowly and methodically dismantled beliefs and barriers that had jammed my system, I gained a new sense of myself. I paid close attention to each part. I was beginning to learn the truth about myself, my past, my pain, and the role I played in becoming a woman in debt.

The Truth About God

As I continued my search, I also became acutely aware of a deep void at the center of my life—a hole that had been there all along, but that I was just beginning to notice. I was to discover, in the months and years ahead, that this missing element was the truth about God.

Knowing the truth about myself meant nothing without knowing the truth about God. I learned this after following a long spiritual journey that took me from Catholicism to Religious Science and down several paths in between. I attended church services, lectures, workshops, and Bible studies. I read books, listened to tapes, and prayed the best way I knew.

Then one morning after returning from a walk along the ocean near my home, I found the thread of truth I had been searching for all my life without knowing it: Jesus Christ. As I cried out to God in confusion and despair over a troubled second marriage, chaotic finances, and hurting children, I collapsed on the grass in a heap. I realized then that I knew a lot *about* God, but I didn't really *know* him in a personal way—in a way that would make a difference in my life.

That morning God met me exactly where I was. He impressed on my spirit that day Jesus' words from Scripture: "I am the way and the truth and the life. No one comes to the Father except through me" (John 14:6). Suddenly I saw the truth for myself. I needed and wanted the assurance of salvation, forgiveness, and eternal life that only Christ can provide. The experience was real. It was life-changing. It was deeply personal.

Until that moment, I had seen Jesus as a great teacher, the Son of God, a miracle-worker, a healer. But I did not know him as *my* Lord and Savior. I had never fully embraced the truth that he died for *me* so that *my* sins could be forgiven and so that *I* could have life everlasting.

The Truth About Everyone

In the years since, I have seen that without God's truth we cannot fully experience the truth about ourselves in any meaningful and lasting way. We need God's wisdom and grace and mercy as we make a commitment to end our abusive cycles with money.

Without exception, I have seen the women in debt with whom I've talked and prayed make dramatic turns in their lives when they commit themselves and their situations to God.

For many, this is one of the *most* difficult decisions they will ever make. Some were spiritually oppressed as children by parents who used the authority of God to frighten and diminish them. Others were raised in homes where legalism and religious doctrine were more important than the relationship between the child and God. And still others were emotionally or sexually abused by a religious representative, such as a minister, priest, or Sunday school teacher.

For some, God became synonymous with religion, ritual, rules, and regulations that did not allow for the natural spontaneity and curiosity that are a part of being a child. Somewhere during their growing-up years the God of love and forgiveness and grace gave way to an authority figure of harsh judgment and punishment.

In my own life, I spent years trying to please a "presence" I did not know or understand. I attended church most of my life, yet I did not have any sense of comfort or encouragement from the God I tried to worship.

I found him, instead, on a grassy knoll above the Pacific Ocean that December morning when I was at the very bottom of myself. It was a simple visitation by a loving God who called me to himself for the restoration I had longed for. For me that spot will always be holy ground, and that area will always be God's promised land, for it was there that I experienced a new beginning.

I believe each one of us has a deep hunger for the fellowship and forgiveness of God. Women in debt who have been forgiven by husbands, children, parents, and co-workers claim even that is not enough. They are tormented by their wrongdoing until they know with certainty that *God* has forgiven them. I don't know any assurance greater than the saving grace of Jesus Christ.

What the Truth Means in Your Life Today

God meets us where we are. If we come to him in pain, and most people do, he guides us as we walk toward the pain, comforts us while we're in it, and provides the grace and direction we need to move through it. In the Bible, we are reminded to "give all your worries and cares to God, for he cares about what happens to you" (1 Peter 5:7 NLT).

How does a woman in debt begin to tell the truth about herself and learn the truth about God? There are no set rules, religious tracts, or courses of action that are right for everyone. That would be a form of legalism and ritual we are trying to avoid.

But I do believe there is a necessary first step to take in order to get the process going. It starts with *willingness—being willing* to tell and receive the truth. If even being willing is too much for you at this point, then you can start with *being willing* to *become willing.* God will meet you there and provide the guidance and grace for what comes next.

It is my deep conviction that no lasting recovery can occur unless and until we become willing to take action and receive support. Even the first step of the 12-step programs, admitting one's powerlessness over one's life and one's addiction, may be too scary for you at this time. But if you are *willing to become willing,* you will have opened the door to the truth about yourself and your situation, the truth about God, and the truth about the importance of both.

God will lead you from there. In Proverbs 3:6 we are advised, "In all your ways acknowledge him, and he will make your paths straight." I can think of no better words for a hungry heart. If you are ready to take that important first step, stop for a moment now and tell God in your own words that you are willing—or at the very least that you are willing to become willing—to tell and receive the truth.

Asking for Help

You may have identified with many of the women you read about in this book. You may have related to their drive to shop or gamble or over-spend or to enable others to use money compulsively. You may also be wondering how to go about changing the course of your own negative behavior once you are willing to change. How can you experience and apply the truths you are discovering?

Dr. Carla Perez, a psychiatrist in San Francisco who has worked with compulsive spenders and shoppers, claims: "You have to start to attack the problem by interrupting either the trigger or the opportunity. Resolving the emotional conflicts that cause the addiction can take a very long time. But while you're working on the emotional trigger, you can take practical steps to interrupt the opportunity."[1]

I agree. But I also believe that the practical steps you take need to be rooted in spirituality if they are to have any permanent value. To tell a woman to buy only what she needs, or to go to a movie instead of a gam-bling casino, or to cut up her credit cards is not a solution. It may work for a time, but when the compulsive urge comes over her again or when the pain in her life becomes severe, she will overspend, gamble, or shop, regardless of her commitment to do otherwise.

The important first step in committing to a new direction is admit-ting you have a problem, acknowledging that you're powerless to change on your own, and then asking God for his help and his wisdom in finding a support system that is best for you. That might include a number of options: private therapy with a counselor who specializes in addictive behaviors (particularly issues with money), group therapy with other women in debt, or one of the 12-step support programs such as Debtors Anonymous or Gamblers Anonymous.

Asking for help means taking some affirmative action on your behalf. If you are not ready to attend a meeting or find a counselor, you might continue reading. Perhaps this is your first book on money abuse. You may wish to read others, some of which I've listed in the back of this book. Or you may reach out for telephone help through a prayer ministry, a crisis hot-line, or simply a trusted friend to share your feelings with.

If you do decide to commit to Debtors Anonymous or other program, or to meet with a counselor or coach, be sure that you give each experience enough time to work. Asking for help implies a level of trust that requires you to let go of your controlling behavior and surrender to a process that will include the influence and support of one or more persons. I encourage you to look for a counselor who understands the importance of spirituality. Choose someone who will be respectful and sympathetic to your views and goals and who is familiar with the destructive cycle you want to break.

Putting yourself in the care of another human being can be a very frightening experience for a woman who already feels out of control. But give yourself and your counselor a chance. Take a deep breath and whisper a prayer to God as you understand him right now, and then *trust*. The Bible says that God knows our every need even before we ask him. What a comforting thought! He will lead us in the paths we must go, if we but ask.

You may also be wondering *why* it is important to ask for help. It's important because you've already tried to do it on your own and that didn't work. You've already made a million promises you didn't keep, and you have already borrowed, loaned, spent, charged, or gambled your way into debt time and again. If you had a cavity you wouldn't try to fill your tooth yourself. If you needed a new set of brakes for your car, chances are you would not attempt to install them on your own. So why struggle alone with something as important as your life? Help is out there. Ask and you will receive.

You may be one who already has a solid belief in God and a loving relationship with him. That's great! Humans are social as well as spiritual beings. God intended us to relate to one another. Frequently, he speaks to us through other people. Without support from others, we may fall into our old ways. We become unwilling and, eventually, unable to see what is really going on. Assume that your situation is worse than you can see or imagine it to be. Ask for help even if you don't think you need it. At the very least, you will receive encouragement for the progress you are making. And at the very most, you will discover how needy you are and will welcome the help that is available.

12
It's Not About Money After All

Women who are overcoming their abuse of money soon discover that the *real* issues they face are not about money after all. Spending plans, repayment of debts, earning, saving, and managing money—essential as they are to reversing destructive behaviors—are not the most important steps toward change.

True change is about entrusting our lives and our situations to God. It's about getting ourselves right spiritually and emotionally so we can use the practical tools in a God-directed way. It's about laying up treasures in heaven, not on earth, "for where your treasure is, there your heart will be also" (Matthew 6:21).

Prayer, the life and breath of the spiritual life, is undoubtedly the means to that goal. A life without prayer is a life without power.

Richard Foster, author of *Celebration of Discipline,* says that prayer "brings us into the deepest and highest work of the human spirit. Real prayer is life creating and life changing."[1] It is through prayer and meditation that we experience the quieting presence of God, commune with him on a personal level, and hear his guidance. If we are committed to being transformed, we will be committed to prayer. Prayer is also the gateway to the spiritual disciplines—the paths by which we enter the life of the spirit. In this chapter, I invite you to look at seven disciplines and how to practice them as you move forward.

Whenever we embark on a new journey, we may be tempted to follow the map so closely that we miss the lovely surprises along the way. God may encourage us to pluck a daisy from the side of the road or contemplate a waterfall on a distant mountain. Be ready for these serendipitous delights. Hold your map loosely! Unknowingly we may also turn the suggestions and invitations here into laws, and then hold ourselves and others accountable to these standards. But we can rest assured that God will help us if that happens, for he has promised he will never leave us nor forsake us. He asks that we lean on his understanding, not our own: "I will instruct you and teach you in the way you should go; I will counsel you and watch over you" (Psalm 32:8).

Recovering from Spiritual Bankruptcy

Many hurting women have no idea how spiritually bankrupt they are. They cannot even imagine life without struggle. But the very moment we declare our willingness to recover from spiritual bankruptcy, we enter the healing process. "Come to me, all you who are weary and burdened, and I will give you rest" (Matthew 11:28). What a comforting promise! What we carried for so long will now be God's. Think of it. God will close the old account and open a new one in partnership with him—a spiritual bank account that deals in the currency of seven spiritual disciplines: study, surrender, service, solitude, simplicity, solvency, and serenity. Many of the disciplines are familiar. We have read about them, wrestled with them, even practiced them from time to time.

Some of us may have held back, assuming these disciplines are too challenging or time-consuming for women who must care for families, raise children, tend homes, or work in the marketplace. Others may have admired them from afar, assigning them to mystics and contemplatives who spend their lives in prayer and fasting. On the contrary, the disciplines of the spiritual life are God's gifts to every woman. In fact, it is on the ordinary streets of life that he does his most transforming work.

I believe that more than ever before, our world needs women who not only practice the disciplines but embrace them, not as an expression of legalism, but as an affirmation of a spirit who truly knows God as her source, her support, her very supply. I hope you choose to be among them.

The Discipline of Study

What Study Means

I believe the most important discipline we can commit to in the initial phase of recovery is *study*. The apostle Paul, in his letter to the Romans, says transformation comes about through the renewing of the mind (see Romans 12:2).

Those of us who have suffered from spiritual abuse, addictions, and compulsive behavior with money need our minds renewed and transformed. Attitudes of hopelessness, negative thinking, and low self-worth have kept many of us from God's guidance. A season of committed study can open the path to His transforming grace and lead to the next discipline—surrender.

To study is to learn by examining, analyzing, investigating, reading and thinking, concentrating, and understanding a piece of written work such as a book or journal. As we study and think, we form thoughts about the object. As a body of knowledge and perceptions takes root in our minds, it becomes the basis for our actions. We are reminded in Proverbs 23:7 that as a man "thinks in his heart, so is he" (NKJV). It is up to us, then, to choose with care, the material we study and reflect on. As Paul reminds us, "Whatever is true, whatever is noble, whatever is right, whatever is pure, whatever is lovely, whatever is admirable—if anything is excellent or praiseworthy—think about such things" (Philippians 4:8).

How to Practice Studying

The most inspiring and useful book for study is the Bible. It is a handbook for life, providing the most complete selection of all that is true, noble, right, pure, lovely, and admirable—from the creation of life to the revelation of life to come. There is a difference, however, between *studying* the Bible and reading it for inspiration and comfort. Studying is searching a passage for its meaning, concentrating on a word or phrase until you see the truth of it, discovering the intention of the author, and finding and holding fast to God's message. Studying is applying your mind. It is a task and function of the intellect. Reading for inspiration and devotion has more to do with basking in the warm glow of God's promises and allowing your spirit to meditate on the things of God for strength and provision.

Other objects of study might include reference books, such as dictionaries and encyclopedias, anthologies on topics of interest, fiction that uplifts and inspires, and nonfiction that instructs, encourages, and provides practical application of a set of instructions or principles that will help us lead more worthwhile lives.

We can apply the discipline of study to our issues with money, as well. If we want to create a spending plan that works, or talk with our creditors, or make informed choices about a job search, a bank account, or an interview, we will need to study these things. New ways of responding to old patterns will not simply emerge fully perfected. They must be pulled down from the shelf, examined, and put into practice.

This discipline also requires a willingness to make ourselves the object of our study so that we might really see our patterns and prejudices, our beliefs and boundaries. Without attending to ourselves, we run the risk of continuing down the same paths while expecting different results.

For some of us, the discipline of study may include returning to school for a college degree in order to begin a new profession or to pursue an interest in a foreign language, in nature and the wilderness, or in travel or real estate or medicine. Studying involves a deep conviction and commitment to personal renewal. It is more than the mere reading of a book or contemplation of our lives or the creation around us. Studying is aligning with the truth and trusting that, as God promised through Jesus, "then you will know the truth, and the truth will set you free" (John 8:32).

Once we know the truth of God's Word, we can move into the next discipline—*surrender*—without hesitation.

The Discipline of Surrender

What Surrender Means

Women who are familiar with 12-step programs know the importance of the third step: "[We] made a decision to turn our wills and our lives over to the care of God as we understood Him."[2] No lasting transformation can occur in our lives without giving control to a power greater than we are. And yet no discipline has been more misused by individuals, families, schools, and religious leaders. Parents demand that children submit to their authority. Warring nations demand surrender of the weaker party to the stronger party or that wrong should surrender to right. Surrender has a bad reputation. In some circles, it suggests a form of bondage, a giving away of all that is valuable and dear and unique to the individual. And no wonder. Many of us have been forced to surrender, made to submit, humiliated into subordination as children, wives, employees, even friends.

The *discipline* of surrender, however, has nothing to do with bondage. It is an expression of freedom. Giving up is *releasing to God* for his safekeeping those people and situations we have no control over anyway. Surrender releases us from carrying the burden of the process as well as the results. We can then walk in freedom, knowing with absolute certainty that the God of the universe, the One who knows all things, who is for all time, will bring about in our lives what is right and good and pure and just, not only in the financial realm, but in every area of our lives.

How to Practice Surrender

The discipline of surrender liberates us. But it also challenges us to express it in accordance with God's will. The danger is in over-spiritualizing it, and thus missing its great gifts. Surrender must never be used to manipulate others or to gain spiritual authority over them. The it's-out-of-my-hands-so-don't-expect-anything-from-me mentality has no place in this discipline.

God-directed surrender suggests that we first submit to his authority and will for our lives. It can be as simple as declaring your willingness in prayer when you awaken in the morning. You might say something as simple as the following:

> *God, today I surrender my whole self to you—everything I think and say and do. Cause me to do your will and to be a blessing to myself and to everyone I come in contact with today.*

After we start our day by surrendering to God in prayer, we will be ready to surrender to our families. That means being available, gently making our presence known and felt, listening and caring, and making it clear that each person matters.

As we move from home to community, we will surely find opportunities to surrender to neighbors and friends, to co-workers, and to those who are downtrodden, sick, and alone, as well as to those who live on the fringes of society. Is there a way we can surrender something useful of our own to someone in need? Even a prized possession, perhaps? Could we surrender a portion of our time to pray with the sick? To shop for the elderly? To help someone move into a new home? To provide food for the hungry?

And we must not forget our place in the world at large, our responsibility to surrender self-centered needs for the greater good of our planet, whether through wilderness conservation, animal protection, or curbing our use of precious natural resources. Those of us who have held ourselves or others hostage through money can surrender our financial obsessions and then reach out to others with similar needs.

In fact, we cannot fully practice the discipline of surrender without combining it with service. The two work together. Surrender without service is akin to telling a hungry woman you'll pray for her without first giving her some bread. And service without true surrender is a work of the flesh and will most certainly lead to burn-out.

If our first act of surrender each day is to God himself, then we can proceed, confident that he will direct us to the places and people he has planned for us to serve.

The Discipline of Service

What Service Means

Women who are trying to give up codependence are understandably wary when it comes to the discipline of service. At first they may see it as the doormat discipline because they have, for so long, allowed others to wipe their shoes on them. But true service is far from that. Service that springs from the heart and soul is a gift of self.

Serving is giving something of yourself to another through money, material goods, a listening ear, a prayer, a portion of time, a talent, or a treasure. One who serves from the spirit knows when to say yes and when to say no. She knows what part is hers and what part belongs to another because she lives with one eye and ear attuned to the natural realm and one eye and ear fixed on the spiritual.

Practice Service Today

In service we must again turn to God for direction through prayer and meditation. True service is not self-serving. It is self-giving. And most importantly, it is God-directed.

For many years I was unclear about how this principle worked. I knew the value of sharing my time and talent with others—from Scout leader to classroom aide, from volunteer at a crisis center to Sunday school teacher. But I had no sense of balance. Like everything else in my life, I served compulsively. I had a lot of "should" attached to it.

I didn't see that true service is rooted in the heart, not in the hands. I assumed that every call to serve was a call on my life. I measured my worth by the amount of time and work I donated each month until I nearly collapsed from burn-out. Then guilt set in. It didn't occur to me to pray about each situation before committing to it; that is, until one illuminating week while teaching a writing course at a camp in the Sierra Mountains.

I laid out my pain and conflict before God one day while walking in the woods. His response was swift and clear. He had called me *to write* and *to teach* and *to pray* according to his will for me, not according to my agenda. I can still recall the incredible rush of relief I felt the moment I took in this clear and direct message.

He then confirmed his words through Scripture and through other people I spoke with during the week. I came to realize that I could contribute to marriages, homeless children, resource conservation, and communication in relationships—subjects I feel passionately about—by writing books about them. And I was to pray for the people he directed me to and in the way he led me. That was another liberating experience. I didn't have to make the decisions about what to do or whom to spend time with or which writing projects to accept or reject. My work life was transformed that week, and I've been at peace about it ever since.

That same clarity is available to each one of us. When our service is God-directed, there will be no struggle. We don't need to prove our worth, earn awards, make our mark, achieve recognition, or drive ourselves to exhaustion. What is done in secret will be rewarded in heaven—where it truly matters.

The Discipline of Silence

What Silence Means

Most people think of *silence* as the absence of sound. But as a spiritual discipline, silence is much more than that. It is also a presence—God's presence in quiet communion with our presence.

Simply refraining from speaking, however, is to miss the gift of wisdom that God has for those who listen for his voice in the silence.

In repentence and rest is your salvation… (Isaiah 30:15).

Be still, and know that I am God (Psalm 46:10).

I will lead the blind by ways they have not known (Isaiah 42:16).

Despite these encouraging words, most of us are so fearful of being silent that we carry around our familiar blanket of noise wherever we go. We depend on the hum of radios and tape decks in our cars, our CD players, televisions, and DVD players in our homes, and cassette players on our waists as we walk or run.

For many of us silence is a fearful thing, an intruder. Perhaps as a little girl you were punished with silence. If you did a bad thing, your parents gave you the silent treatment, or you were sent to your room to stay there in silence, or you were told to hush or keep your mouth shut. Or if you come from a large, noisy household, you may have longed for a few moments of silence but never got them. Or perhaps you craved a time of solitude under a tree, or by a river bank, or in a secret hideaway, where you could think and dream and write or listen to the birds or pray.

As an adult it may be painful for you to even consider carving out a time of silence. You may not know what to do with it or how to benefit from it. The moment you sit down with yourself and your thoughts, you might suddenly remember an e-mail you must send, a load of clothes that needs washing, a stack of lessons that needs correcting, a pile of bills that needs paying.

Silence is not an easy discipline to embrace. We talk about it, think of it, and wish for it, but rarely do we experience it. Entering silence requires a step of faith, a commitment to nurture ourselves, a willingness to stop the noise and see what's on the other side. It also requires that we practice being alone, moving into a space of solitude, where we can listen and hear and experience the comfort and power of God within us.

Susannah Wesley, mother of 19 children—among them John, the founder of Methodism, and Charles, a famous hymn writer—spent two hours a day in silence and prayer, and this was in the 1700s, long before microwave ovens and clothes dryers and daycare.

It is one thing to be inspired by the practice of others, and quite another to be motivated for ourselves. All of the disciplines require courage and commitment, but perhaps silence and solitude more than any others. We depend on words. To be without them can make us feel defenseless. But silence calls us to stop the self-talk, the mindless head chatter, the rational thinking, the planning, and the manipulation that make up so much of our lives. We can practice silence. And when our ideas and dreams demand a hearing; when guilt, worry, and doubt compete for attention; when problems shout for a solution, we can whisper, "Hush. I'm waiting on God. In quietness and trust is my salvation."

And if we persist, oh, the treasures of the spirit we will receive! Pretense and apology will disappear. Familiar burdens will become unimportant. Our need to control people and events will give way to the steadying hand of God. And we will begin to let go of our stockpile of jealousy, anger, fear, pride, and bitterness.

Wisely, the writer of Ecclesiastes says there is "a time to be silent and a time to speak" (3:7). Those of us who wish to practice the discipline of silence will heed those words.

How to Practice Silence

How do we find quiet in a noisy world? How do we get *there* from *here?* First, we can take hold of small swatches of time as they appear. Find a place, or create one, where you can be alone and enter silence. One woman I know has "lunch with the Lord." She brings her food in a brown bag and finds a spot under a tree near her office where she eats and reflects, writes in her journal, or simply sits in silence for the hour she has each day.

Next, we can choose a time and put it on the calendar like any other engagement. You might commit one Saturday a month to a silent retreat when you go away physically—to a park, a church, the woods, or the sea, and renew yourself in silence. You might consider fasting at one mealtime each week and using that time to commune with yourself and God in silence. Small pockets of inner silence are also possible first thing in the morning as we awaken and lie quietly in our beds or the last thing at night before dropping off to sleep.

During the day we can enter inner silence while standing in line at the post office or the bank or sitting in a doctor's waiting room. Even with the noise of others around us, we can learn to turn our spiritual ears to the things of God. Once we have experienced this inner silence, the world cannot so easily disrupt us again. We know what it is to be still and to know God.

And what fruit the tree of silence bears! We will grow up as our inner persons are changed and as we give up the need to speak everything that is on our minds, of the desire to set the record straight, of the compulsion to tell others what to do and how to behave. We will suddenly notice that we have the ability to solve our financial and other problems without struggle. Leading and guidance will be there at the precise moments we need them. We will experience the release of creative expression and, perhaps most important, an abiding sense of trust and awareness of God's presence at *all* times.

The Discipline of Simplicity
What Simplicity Means

Simplicity is an absence of ornament, of show and pretense; it is freedom from useless accessories. What an exercise in discipline this could be for those of us who have bound ourselves to shopping and overspending and abusing credit cards. But what a great gust of cleansing wind it could be, as well, if we were to greet it with enthusiasm. And to those who have found their worth through gambling and enabling others to go into debt, the discipline of simplicity offers the opportunity to find our worth on the inside instead of on the outside.

For women who push money away through self-debt, under-earning, and pauperism, a life of simplicity can restore a sense of dignity and purpose and balance. We can choose to live our lives free of materialism, free of the need to *prove* our value by denying ourselves even the necessities. As the familiar Shaker hymn reminds us, "'Tis a gift to be simple, 'Tis a gift to be free. 'Tis a gift to come down where we ought to be." For many women in debt, coming down to where they ought to be would be a gift indeed. Coming down from fantasy to reality, from grandiosity to sincerity, from dishonesty to honesty where they can live in both prudence and plenty.

Simplicity is not austerity, which renounces the things of the world. Instead, it puts things in proper perspective. Simplicity encourages us to be well, look well, feel well, and do well without making a statement about it. Simplicity allows us to drive an old car because we want to, not because we have to. Or to drive a new car because we want to, not because we have to. Like the apostle Paul, we can be content in plenty or in want because simplicity, like all the disciplines, begins on the inside. When we are simple within, we are free without.

"Simplicity," says Richard Foster, "sets us free to receive the provision of God as a gift that is not ours to keep, and that can be freely shared with others."[3]

Simplicity in Your Life Today

Even the desire for a simple lifestyle cannot take precedence over our relationship with God or it too can become an addiction! Simplicity means taking our hands off the controls and depending on God, as do the birds of the air and the lilies of the field.

Practicing simplicity involves trust and prudence. For women in debt, this may be a challenging step that requires the prayer and support and wisdom of caring people before and after we make decisions about how to spend or save or invest our money.

A simpler life includes learning how to make wise choices about our clothing and transportation and housing needs. Do you really need 15 pairs of shoes? Can you enjoy your clothing for several seasons, rather than answering the call to every fashion trend that comes along? Are you willing to live in a modest dwelling that is affordable and comfortable, rather than a showplace that drains your earnings each month?

Simplicity encourages us to modify our diets, to embrace simple, nourishing foods that we can prepare at home and share with others instead of cramming fast food into our mouths while we drive or read the paper or finish a report at work.

The simple life also embraces caring and consciousness about the earth and its resources. If you use paper goods, you may want to consider replacing them with washable, recyclable materials.

Simplifying could mean clearing out the physical and emotional clutter in our lives—from old magazines to old friends who no longer nourish us. Do we really need to subscribe to every publication that interests us? Must we have our own washer and dryer, CD player, and a television in every room? Or could we take advantage of these items and services available through community resources such as the public library and neighborhood laundry? How liberating it can be to use something without owning it. Wouldn't it be lovely to be free of dusting items we don't need, fixing things that continue to break, replacing equipment that wears out?

My husband and I have only recently discovered this truth for ourselves. We live in a wonderful condominium near the ocean. The location is ideal for our lifestyle, and the rooms are generous in size. We have a delightful public park nearby, and we can walk or run along the beach every day if we wish. The post office, library, church, grocery stores, and other businesses are all within a short drive or walk.

Some professionals believe that buying a house would be a better investment. During our healing process with money issues, however, we both realized that if we are pleased by this place, if it meets our needs and desires and satisfies the criteria we have for a home, then it is a *good* investment, regardless of what anyone else thinks.

The discipline of simplicity can also be applied to our inner life. For example, we can streamline our prayers so that God does more of the talking and we do more listening. We could also heed his command to pray without ceasing by making our lives a prayer chain, each link connected by short one-line prayers of praise and petition throughout the day: "Lord, watch over me in the meeting today." "Lord, thank you for that delicious lunch." "God, I need your strength tonight." "Father God, I know that you are providing for my every need."

Simplicity: The discipline that brings us down to where we ought to be so we can move into a solvent lifestyle.

The Discipline of Solvency

What Solvency Means

Solvency—the ability to pay all that one owes—is the goal of all women in debt who desire real freedom. But there remains for many of us a great gap between the desire and the reality. That is when 12-step programs and other support groups can be so helpful. In these meetings, you can share your tragedies and your triumphs and be heard, understood, and loved.

The discipline of solvency challenges us to discover our needs and wants, to bring them into perspective in terms of what is real and true in our lives—such as earnings, the season of our lives, the status of our households and dependent family members—and then bring all of this before God for his guidance and blessing.

Solvency Today

Solvency is not a discipline that a woman in debt can practice without support. What has taken a lifetime to dismantle cannot be restored through sheer willpower. But we can take the initial steps that prepare us for the support of others by confronting *our* patterns with money. I know of no better avenue than Debtors Anonymous for this first step toward living a solvent life. There you will receive the practical guidance and encouragement you'll need to create a spending plan, talk to your creditors, and make amends to those you've hurt financially. You will also receive the emotional and spiritual support you'll need to tackle the deeper issues that are the true cause of your financial compulsions.

I believe solvency and simplicity are closely connected. Simplicity provides a solid foundation on which solvency can be practiced. When a woman in debt embraces simplicity, she says to herself and others that she is committed to freeing herself of the tangles of the world. And when that commitment takes place deep within her, she will begin to practice solvency almost without realizing it.

Solvency, like the other disciplines, is "an inside job." What occurs in the spiritual realm will show up in the natural realm as soon as a woman commits to living her life free of debt. Such women earn, save, share, spend, and invest out of a deep conviction, based on God's guidance, of what is right and true and just.

Practicing solvency in our lives also includes a willingness to learn all we can about practical financial matters that affect our everyday affairs. It means we take an interest in managing checking accounts, handling cash in responsible ways, planning for future needs and wants, setting aside funds for emergencies, investments, vacations, and retirement.

It includes praying for guidance about who to speak with, which seminars to attend, what books to read and tapes to listen to. The discipline of solvency is the outworking of an inward commitment to become good stewards of the resources God provides.

A solvent lifestyle results in a deep peace that paves the way for a life of serenity.

The Discipline of Serenity

What Serenity Means

Serenity is a state of calm, of peace, a deep inner knowing that all is well. This is the plane of life we most desire. Thankfully, serenity is not tied to any one practice or any one area of life. It is, instead, a spiritual discipline that brings about a state of total well-being as a woman comes to rest in God. To be serene is to be accepting, to hold life, self, and other people with an open hand instead of a clenched fist.

Practice Serenity

I cannot think of a better way to practice serenity than to live the words of the Serenity Prayer:

> God, grant me the serenity to accept the things I cannot change, the courage to change the things I can, and the wisdom to know the difference.[4]

Individuals who live these words no longer lean on themselves or the things of the world. They know that their personal power is limited and that they are effective only to the extent that God empowers them. They do not waste time trying to figure out what to do, what to say, or how to respond. They go to God *first*. And they ask for the power they need to accept whatever comes at them that they cannot change. Then they ask for the courage to change what they can. This takes some doing because it implies that they will be given the knowledge of what they can change, and they must then do it.

Finally, and most important, they seek the wisdom they need to know the difference between the two. Without wisdom, their serenity would be jeopardized. In all cases, they come before God, leaning on his power and understanding, not on their own. And in so doing they release the results to him, as well, further ensuring their serenity and the right and just outworking of God in the lives of those around them. What freedom!

Streams in the Desert

As we take up the spiritual journey, we can turn to the disciplines like streams in a desert that refresh our spirits when we feel dry and guide us when we feel lost. And for those times when we feel strong and sure-footed, the disciplines enable us to explore new terrain with the confidence that God is with us every step of the way.

As we *study* the things of the spirit and the world, we become aware of our own limitations. This leads to *surrender* to God. As we surrender, we are drawn into *service,* so that we might reach out to others and in turn share God's gifts and guidance.

In order to serve with power and purpose, it is necessary for us to refresh and refuel ourselves with *silence* and to draw away from the world in *solitude,* where we can meet God in meditation and prayer. As we become sensitive to God's voice, we begin to see the wisdom of his word in Scripture to live *in* the world but not *of* the world. And this helps us take our emphasis off material things and embrace the spiritual gift of *simplicity.*

Solvency, then, becomes the natural outflow of a simple, clutter-free life. And when a woman is free to study, surrender, and serve without hindrance, to embrace silence, simplicity, and solvency without question, she will naturally and supernaturally live in a state of *serenity.*

At times the streams may seem to disappear in the vast sea of sand around us, and we may feel our spirits go dry. But if God has given us certain talents and longings, we can be certain they have something to do with our ultimate purpose in life. To attain that purpose, let us commit to our goals and then live disciplined lives in order to accomplish them.

> For the LORD God is a sun and shield; the LORD bestows favor and honor; no good thing does he withhold from those whose walk is blameless (Psalm 84:11).

Part 4
Discovering
Joy

13
Building a Support System

As you begin to heal, one of the most important and effective gifts you can give yourself is a *support system*. I have discovered over the past 12 years that I cannot live a productive and serene life without help. I believe God intended us to draw strength and joy from one another. The Bible tells us that when there is no guidance people fall, but there is victory for those who seek the counsel of many (see Proverbs 11:14).

Now I surround myself with support on every level of my life—spiritual, physical, mental, emotional, social, and financial. Following are some suggestions, based on my experience and that of other women in recovery, that may be of help to you as you build your own support system.

Stay Connected to People

The tendency of women with money problems is to withdraw when we are in pain. I urge you to reach out to others and stay connected.

Join a 12-step program such as Debtors Anonymous or Gamblers Anonymous. These and other 12-step groups are based on the original 12 steps of Alcoholics Anonymous (AA), which has been responsible for millions of people worldwide achieving and maintaining sobriety. Even though these groups have adapted AA's program to problems other than alcoholism, and in doing so do not imply that AA either approves or endorses their adaptations or programs, Debtors Anonymous (DA) and

Gamblers Anonymous (GA) offer the same kind of opportunity for those who want to achieve and maintain solvency.

Overcomers Outreach is also patterned after AA, but is designed for Christian believers who look specifically to *Jesus Christ* as their higher power. This 12-step group welcomes people with every kind of addiction—either process or chemical—and is committed to studying Scripture as it relates to the 12 steps and to praying for the needs of each individual.

Many Christians feel this group, founded by Bob and Pauline Bartosch, has done more for Christians in recovery than any other group. Overcomers Outreach does not deal with money issues in the same focused way that DA and GA do. However, some people attend both groups and find this an effective way to meet their practical and spiritual needs. They work with the tools of DA or GA and receive Christ-centered support from Overcomers Outreach.

One of the most valuable tools offered in DA and GA is something called the Pressure Relief Group (PRG), designed to help you take pressure off yourself. Typically a PRG consists of you and two others, usually a man and a woman. A meeting of the group might last one to two hours. During this time you have the opportunity to lay out your financial situation, discuss options for debt repayment, and set up a realistic spending plan—one that includes money to share with a charity or church of your choice and money for things that bring you happiness and a sense of well-being. For one woman it might be fresh flowers; for another, it might be a membership in a health club; for one it might be a meal out; or another, a movie once a week.

The idea is to make room in your spending plan for charitable giving such as tithing a portion of your income to an organization or church of your choice and making room for yourself—not just for your creditors. Members of DA are committed to repaying *all* debts. Bankruptcy is never encouraged or endorsed. Through bitter experience, most members have come to realize that unless they take care of themselves first, they will not have the stamina or the resources to pay what they owe. The spending plan allows for both. You will also receive suggestions and guidance on how to contact your creditors to consult with them regarding your repayment plans.

Typical meetings of 12-step programs last about an hour and include an opening prayer, announcements, pertinent readings, and voluntary sharing. Members of the group speak individually for three to five minutes or longer if needed about their struggles with money issues and their personal progress. It is a safe and sane environment in which to listen, share, and learn.

Another resource that is growing in popularity is Crown Financial Ministries founded by the late Larry Burkett and Howard Dayton, currently the chief executive officer. This Christian-based organization is committed to "teaching people God's financial principles" through seminars, literature, and outreach. See the list of resources in the back of the book for contact information for all the groups mentioned.

Find a Support Partner

A helpful facet of these programs is sponsorship. Sponsors are people who have been in the program for six months or more and are practicing solvency "one day at a time." Newcomers are encouraged to ask someone to be their sponsor. They can then turn to those people for support and guidance as they move through the 12 steps of the program.

Another option I have found beneficial in my life is teaming up with a friend for the purpose of mutual support. For the past four years I have been involved in a prayer partnership with my friend and writing colleague Mona. We e-mail our prayer needs to each other once a week and then uphold one another in prayer each day that week.

My friend Dianna, whom I met at church, has been my personal prayer partner for nearly 20 years. We talk and pray with each other by phone several times a month. Our life histories are very similar, so we have become for each other a safe haven where we are listened to and loved no matter what. The healing power of these special times cannot be measured in words. I feel totally blessed at the end of each of our sessions.

And, of course, those of us who are married can turn to our spouses for encouragement and accountability on a daily basis.

Seek Advice

If I want to make a major purchase, invest a sum of money, buy an insurance policy, plan a trip, or make a business-related financial decision, I call people I have connected with in business or through my support groups and talk over the details before taking action. I also consult with my husband before any major financial outlay. After all these years, we are true partners in every way.

Those of us with a history of denial, guilt, and grandiosity regarding money need the counsel of many. I find that talking through the process helps me discover where I am being unrealistic and imprudent or wise and thoughtful. Sometimes just a question or a shared experience from the other party provides the balance I need. There is nothing like a good sounding board.

Start a Journal

About 15 years ago when I was in deep pain over my money and marital issues, I approached a counselor friend at the church I attend. He listened to me patiently, offered some encouragement, and then suggested that I begin keeping a journal. I was hesitant at first, but then decided to try it for a month. I've been journaling ever since.

The thing I like most about writing in a journal is that there is no one way to do it. It is as individual as each person. You can record events and expenses, share your feelings about your money issues, note patterns of spending or shopping or gambling or whatever it is you do, write a letter to God, and create a dialogue with money itself. For example:

> *Karen:* Hi, Money. I feel silly talking to an inanimate object, but someone suggested I try this in order to relieve the tension I'm feeling in my relationship with you.
>
> *Money:* Good! Nice to hear from you. What's on your mind?
>
> *Karen:* You are. Day and night. I can't get along with you. I can't get along without you. What's going on?

Money: Hey, don't blame me. I'm an inanimate object, remember? You're the one who calls the shots, not me....

And so on. In just one 5-minute writing session, I discovered that I had given money a God-like status in my life, when in fact money itself is powerless without my direction. Journaling was a powerful experience, and I have repeated the process on many occasions to defuse out-of-control feelings and to gain clarity. I recommend journaling. Just begin and see where it takes you.

Affirm the Positive

An affirmation is a positive thought or statement you consciously repeat to affirm the truth. For example: *I, Karen, earn, manage, and share money through the power of God within me for the good of everyone concerned.* Whether we realize it or not, many of us affirm and confirm our financial condition by the words we speak: *"I can't afford it." "I hate money; I've never understood it." "I don't have money for that right now."* These self-defeating messages actually create our reality.

We have more power than we know. Instead of affirming the negative, affirm the positive and feed your spirit messages of hope and encouragement. For example: *"Today I open myself to learning one new thing about money." "Money is my friend." "Money is coming my way as God provides for my every need."*

You may also wish to use Jesus' teaching on abundance as the basis for your affirmations. I can't think of anything more spiritually health-giving than to feed on the Word of God.

My purpose is to give life in all its fullness (John 10:10 TLB).

The Lord will work out his plans for my life—for your loving-kindness, Lord, continues forever (Psalm 138:8 TLB).

But seek first his kingdom and his righteousness, and all these things will be given to you as well (Matthew 6:33).

> But remember the LORD your God, for it is he who gives you the ability to produce wealth (Deuteronomy 8:18).

I like to insert my name into these passages to make them personal. Try it for yourself and see how it feels.

> "My purpose is to give life *to you, Karen,* in all its fullness" (John 10:10).
>
> "*Karen, you shall* remember the LORD your God, for it is he who gives you the ability to produce wealth" (Deuteronomy 8:18).

When I say and hear my name, I am reminded of God's will and love for me. It helps me stay connected to him as the true source of everything I need and want.

Pray and Wait

The apostle Paul counseled the Ephesians to "put on the full armor of God," that they would be able to stand firm against the evil that was all around them (see Ephesians 6:11). Then he reminded them that their struggle was not against flesh and blood but against the powers and principalities of the unseen world. How well those of us who struggle with debt know this to be true!

How often have we tried to become healthy ourselves through the sheer force of our own will—by promising yet another time to stop our self-destructive spending or shopping or gambling or enabling, only to fall again? We can do battle only when we are wearing the armor of God—his shield, his helmet, his sword. Then, after having done all we can, we must stand firm, waiting on God to complete the work he started within us.

Jesus counsels, "if you believe, you will receive whatever you ask for in prayer" (Matthew 21:22). It is up to each of us to discover for ourselves the joy and freedom that await us through prayer—our lifeline to God.

14
Sanity, Serenity, Solvency—
A Way of Life

Do you remember Miki? I shared her under-earner story in chapter 8. When women tell Miki they're not sure they can relate to the spiritual side of life, she is quick to respond, "What other side is there?" She believes compulsions are "the result of a spiritual emptiness that drives us to behave in an insane way." For her, sanity, serenity, and solvency are possible only because of her relationship with God. Through Miki's participation in 12-step programs, she says, "I now have the knowledge and practical tools to handle my money. But only God can remove my compulsions."

Today Miki turns everything in her life over to God—her issues with under-earning and overeating, her relationships with her daughter and husband, and her work life. "God, tell me what to do, and I'll do it," is her daily prayer. "I also know," she says, "that God expects me to do the footwork."

Miki regularly attends two 12-step recovery programs, and she talks and prays with her sponsors each week. She has worked out a spending plan and is looking at ways to increase her income and her standard of living. "This time," she says, "I really want to do it God's way."

One of the things that struck me while talking with Miki and other women, and also thinking about my own life, was the incredibly personal way God has met each one of us. Some, like Miki, have been delivered from self-will. Many have met God through a 12-step program. And others, including me, came into a relationship with him after our lives fell apart. But the important thing is that *God makes himself real to those who seek him.*

Spiritual Snapshots

In this final chapter, I've included a few spiritual snapshots of some of the women you've met in these pages. What do they do to retain their sanity, serenity, and solvency? How do they relate to God? How does he reveal himself in their lives?

Some women, like Marcie, whose issue is self-debting, are still exploring their spirituality. Others, like Anne Marie, who acknowledges herself as a debt enabler, came into recovery with a spiritual foundation. She is now out of debt and making rapid progress earning, saving, and investing.

Marcie is struggling with God as her provider because for so long there was no one to turn to but herself. Today, however, she is feeling more serene as she works through her incest issues in private therapy. "I am also working on the *idea* of a higher power," she says. "I go to spiritual retreats to help me with this. And I use the phone a lot." She calls people for support whenever she has financial decisions to make or when she is feeling weak or vulnerable. Marcie, like all of the women I spoke with, attends regular meetings of various support programs for the sharing and support they offer.

God has softened Nancy's heart since she has begun recovering from alcoholism and debting. "Now I take God into my work and my personal life," she says, her voice glowing with praise. She attends a spiritual service each week and continues to affirm "God will provide."

Kelly, who has struggled with pauperism, says with conviction in her voice, "Knowing God is the most astounding thing that ever happened to me. Today, I align my will with God's and hear him gently telling me there is plenty for me." She is eager to share some of the miracles God has worked in her life regarding financial and spiritual recovery. "I have always had a hard time buying myself the clothes I need," she says. "I usually wore an old T-shirt to bed, but what I really wanted was a beautiful pink nightgown. One day as my husband and I were driving, I noticed something pink lying in the street. I had to stop. My husband pulled over, I jumped out of the car, and there was a pink nightie, embossed, stylish, brand-new. It still had the store tag on it. All I could say was 'Oh, my God!' My breath was taken away." Kelly picked up the nightie, hopped back into the car, and thanked God. "I told him that however he brings things into my life is great with me," she said with a lilt in her voice.

Another time Kelly needed a pair of size 11 low-heeled beige pumps to go with a suit, but she didn't have the money. God delivered again. Her grandmother gave her the exact shoes she desired without even knowing Kelly was in need. "I am such a tangible person, it's been difficult for me to believe in God," Kelly says, but she admits with a big smile that God is removing that difficulty in some pretty awesome ways!

Julie spends many hours a day working on her gift business. But before she begins work each morning, she spends 20 minutes in meditation and an hour walking along the beach near her home. "And then I get down on my knees and say my daily prayers. I hear God whisper, 'I love you, Julie.' God speaks so gently. We have to pay attention or we'll miss him."

Julie also embraces the principles of Debtors Anonymous and attends regular meetings in order to deal with her overspending. "The first time I went I sat there with my arms tightly crossed, and I left feeling angry. I found out that I had a lot of growing up to do." Months later she returned, "and that time I felt the spirituality," she said. "I felt as if I were being welcomed home."

Suzanne, who spent most of her life being taken care of financially by others, is now experiencing being cared for by the one who really matters to her—Jesus Christ. "We're studying the book of James in the women's group I attend at church," she says. "This has helped me so much with the trials and tribulations in my life. I am also in a women's therapy group where we can talk and share our problems with one another. Two of the books we've studied that I recommend highly are *Feeling Good* and *The Feeling Good Handbook* by David Burns, M.D."

When Anne Marie joined Debtors Anonymous (DA), she was grateful to find that the principles of DA are compatible with the Quaker attitudes and beliefs she practices as a member of the Society of Friends. "We believe in being quick to repay debts," she says, "in being good stewards over our possessions, and in living a peace-oriented life." Now she feels she has a proper balance between the practical and the spiritual side of her recovery.

Dianne, also a Quaker, says that even though she attended church every Sunday for 25 years, she still "wrestled with God and was angry with him" over her abusive marriage and unsettling divorce. "But now I see that God doesn't make or not make life easy for us. That depends on how we behave and what we do."

Before entering DA, however, Dianne had "compartmentalized the debting, the enabling, and the abuse. I didn't see that as part of my daily life." She used denial to hide her pain. But today her spiritual life is coming about through a gradual healing with her mother, private therapy, her church support, and Debtors Anonymous.

Roberta is working with a counselor who is helping her with her spiritual program and the core issues that fueled her spending and credit-card abuse. She also keeps a journal and meets with other journal writers every two weeks. The 12-step recovery programs have helped Roberta come to terms with money issues and relationships.

Chris says she has had some true miracles in her life. "After completing 9 of the 12 steps in my program for overeaters, all of the promises the program lists—except the one about money—had come true. But now after over a year in DA, even that promise is being fulfilled. I have hardly any financial insecurity now."

Chris has also stopped debting completely. She has been solvent since she started the program, despite her problems with under-earning. "I am more conscious of asking for God's guidance," she says. "I really believe God wants me to be prosperous. And I feel prosperous now that I am living within my means."

Today Chris is pursuing work in the counseling field, where she was trained and now feels called to work. Chris is grateful for 12-step programs because they have had a major part in her spiritual awakening. "I needed to apply the steps of recovery specifically to money," she says. "I was an atheist before I entered a recovery program 12 years ago. Now I am a believer. God is personal to me, and my faith is strong. I know I can communicate with God whenever I want to. This is the most important thing in my life." Chris's spiritual practices include daily prayer, dialoguing with God, talking with her sponsor, attending meetings, and serving as a sponsor and phone partner for other women with money problems.

Hope and a Future

My own healing process is also filled with the grace of God and the fruit of much hard work. My husband, Charles, and I have joined forces in our war on debt and in our commitment to God.

Charles retired from one of the finest department stores in the country. Thanks to a generous employee discount on all merchandise—available even after retirement—our clothing needs are now fully met, and we are well-dressed. Through the store's profit-sharing program we were able to purchase our own home.

As of 1991, I became debt-free, and for the first time in years I have a savings account, a growing retirement plan, and a fund for taxes and investments. We live a completely solvent lifestyle now, paying cash for everything.

Together we have embraced the discipline of simplicity and have a more prosperous and peaceful life than ever before. We have come to treasure our cozy Saturday night dates at home with a rented movie and simple food. We set aside money for travel, and we plan ahead if we wish to attend a night at the symphony or a matinee performance at a local theater.

We pray each morning, turning our wills and our lives, our families, our finances, and our workplaces over to God. We tithe, and God multiplies that money and brings it back to us. I have almost eliminated worry from my life. I am able now to see the lesson behind the problems and pain in a way I couldn't years ago.

Money has also come into our lives in some wondrous ways: part-time employment for Charles as a tour guide, gifts, pay increases, new writing opportunities, inheritance, surprises such as equity in an insurance policy, speaking engagements, teaching weekends, and through selling books, old records, and other possessions we no longer need or want. I am convinced now that our most basic needs, as well as our most ardent wishes, are as dear to God as we are.

My prayer, as you become free from overspending, compulsive shopping, credit-card abuse, gambling, enabling, under-earning, self-debting, or pauperism is that you will know with certainty that *your* place is not in the mall or in the casino or in debt to a bank. It is truly under the loving and protective arm of God. " 'For I know the plans I have for you,' declares the LORD, 'plans to prosper you and not to harm you, plans to give you hope and a future' " (Jeremiah 29:11).

Supplementary Resources

Books

Celebration of Discipline: The Path to Spiritual Growth, by Richard Foster. Harper & Row, 1988. An inspiring and practical book on the classical spiritual disciplines for anyone who wishes to break free of superficial habits and draw closer to God.

The Challenge of the Disciplined Life, Christian Reflections on Money, Sex, and Power (formerly, *Money, Sex, and Power*), by Richard Foster. Harper & Row San Francisco, 1991. The author explores three of the great themes of everyday life that are of imminent concern to Christians today: money, sex, power, and how "giving" in each area can bring vitality and authenticity to our relationship with God, with ourselves, and with others.

Devotions for Debtors, by Kristin Johnson Ingram. Galilee/Doubleday, 2002. A book of daily devotions with Scripture verses and action steps. Excellent source of strength and hope.

A Good Steward's Journal: The Busy Christian's Guide to Better Money Management, by Kathy Miller. A practical workbook that outlines a system that makes budgeting convenient, easy to understand, and fun. All worksheets are provided in this one volume. Order this and other helpful books directly from Kathy Miller's website: www.agoodsteward.net.

How to Get Out of Debt, Stay Out of Debt, and Live Prosperously (based on the proven principles and techniques of Debtors Anonymous), by Jerrold Mundis. Bantam, 1988. A simple, effective formula for freeing yourself from debt and staying that way.

Pain and Pretending, expanded edition with Study Guide, by Rich Buhler. Thomas Nelson Publishers, 1991. A significant resource on the pain and recovery of victimization by a seasoned counselor, minister, talk-show host, and expert on the topic. An older book, but still available through amazon.com.

Suze Orman's Financial Guidebook: Put the 9 Steps to Work, by Suze Orman. Three Rivers Press, 2002. Reading this book is like having a one-on-one financial planning session with Suze. You may also wish to visit her website: www.suzeorman.com.

When Pleasing Others Is Hurting You, by Dr. David Hawkins. Harvest House, 2004. Wisdom and practical help for those who feel their identity has been lost along the road to winning other people's approval.

Organizations and Support Groups

A Good Steward

An organization founded by Christian prosperity coach Kathy Miller, dedicated to "providing support with getting beyond your current circumstances, going deeper, growing into a better version of yourself, and becoming the person you always wanted to be." Visit Miller's website for more info on her services and products: www.agoodsteward.net.

Christian Credit Help

One of the industry's leading Debt Management Program providers helping individuals and families become debt free. For a FREE consultation, visit the organization's website: www.christiancredithelp.org and fill out a form online.

Consumer Credit Counseling Service

A nonprofit organization that provides budget, credit, and debt counseling *free* of charge. This is not a collection or lending institution. The service helps people help themselves to solve their debt problems. For information about offices in your area or elsewhere in the United States, call their toll-free number:

800-355-2227 or visit their website: http://www.cccservices.com/home.asp.

Crown Financial Ministries

PO Box 100
Gainesville, GA 30503-0100
Products and Materials: 800-722-1976
General: 770-534-1000
Website: www.crown.org

A Christian-based organization dedicated to helping people learn and practice God's financial principles. For more information contact the head office or visit the website.

Debtors Anonymous General Service Board

General Service Office
PO Box 920888
Needham, MA 02492-0009
Telephone: 781-453-2743
Fax: 781-453-2745
www.debtorsanonymous.org

For information about meetings in your area, and how to get started on a program of recovery, contact the office or visit the organization's website.

Gamblers Anonymous International Service Office

PO Box 17173
Los Angeles, CA 90017
Telephone: 213-386-8789
Fax: 213-386-0030
www.gamblersanonymous.org
isomain@gamblersanonymous.org

For information about meetings in your area and how to get started on a program of recovery, contact the office or visit the organization's website.

National Council on Problem Gambling

208 G Street, NE
Washington, D.C. 20002
Telephone: 202-547-9204
Fax: 202-547-9206
E-mail: ncpg@ncpgambling.org
Helpline Network: 1-800-522-4700

For information about one of the 33 state affiliate programs, contact the office or visit the website.

Overcomers Outreach

PO Box 2208
Oakhurst, CA 93644
Phone Toll Free: 1-800-310-3001
www.overcomersoutreach.org
Email: info@overcomersoutreach.org

For information about meetings in your area, how to get started on a program of recovery with a Christ-centered approach, or how to establish a group in your church, contact the office or visit the organization's website.

Notes

Chapter 2—Crazy About Money

1. From a phone interview with Kathy Miller and a visit to her website: www.agoodsteward.net. Used with permission.

2. Kathy Miller's workbook, *A Good Steward's Journal*, is available at www.agood steward.net.

Chapter 3—A woman's Place Is in the Mall—Overspenders

1. From an in-person interview with Sharene Garaman. Used with permission.

Chapter 4—Born to Shop—Shopaholics

1. Connie Jasper, "Addicted to Shopping," http://home.earthlink.net/~conny jasper/id2.html.

Chapter 5—Maxed Out—Credit-Card Abusers

1. Liz Pulliam Weston, http://moneycentral.msn.com/content/ SavingandDebt/P74808.asp.

Chapter 6—A Dollar and a Dream—Compulsive Gamblers

1. From an e-mail interview with Dr. Perkinson and from his website: http://www.robertperkinson.com. Used with permission.

2. From information gathered from the website of the National Council on Problem Gambling, http://www.ncpgambling.org/ about_problem/about_problem_fact.asp.

3. Mark Sauer, "Show of Hands," *San Diego Union-Tribune*, August 22, 2004, Section E, p. 1.

4. From an article at http://www.femalegamblers.org/past-issues/ jan2004.htm.

5. From a telephone interview with Dr. Henry Lesieur, July 1991. Used with permission.

6. Gwenda Blair, "Betting Against the Odds," *New York Times Magazine,* 25 September 1988, 76.

7. Tomas M. Martinez, *The Gambling Scene* (Springfield, IL: Charles C. Thomas, 1983), cited in "The Psychology of Gambling," by Igor Kusyszyn, *The Annals of the American Academy,* July 1984, 137.

Chapter 7—The Great Cover-up—Debt Enablers

1. Robin Norwood, *Women Who Love Too Much* (New York: Pocket Books, 1985).

Chapter 8—Living on the Edge—Under-Earners

1. From Liza Guttierez, "Working Hard, Making Less," *American Observer,* vol. 9, no. 8, website: http://observer.american.edu/ 2004/apr1404/women.html.

2. Ibid.

3. Ibid., citing Linda Babcock and Sara Laschever, *Women Don't Ask* (Princeton University Press, 2003).

4. Ibid.

5. From an in-person interview with Susan McKean. Used with permission.

Chapter 11—Telling and Receiving the Truth

1. From Susan Jacoby, "Compulsive Shopping," *Glamour,* 1986, 350.

Chapter 12—It's Not About Money After All

1. Richard Foster, *Celebration of Discipline* (San Francisco: Harper & Row, 1978), 30.

2. *Alcoholics Anonymous* (New York: Alcoholics Anonymous World Services, Inc., 1976), 59.

3. Foster, *Celebration,* 74.

4. Paraphrase of a prayer composed by Reinhold Niebuhr, cited in *Bartlett's Familiar Quotations* by John Bartlett (Boston: Little, Brown, 1968), 1024. This paraphrase is often used in 12-step programs.

To share how this book has helped you
or to ask Karen O'Connor
to speak to your group or organization,
please contact her at:

www.karenoconnor.com
or
1-800-355-1832

Other Good
Harvest House Reading

THE PRAYER THAT CHANGES EVERYTHING™
Stormie Omartian

Stormie shares personal stories, biblical truths, and practical ideas to reveal the wonders that take place when we offer praise in the middle of difficulties, sorrow, fear, and, yes, abundance and joy. When we are at our weakest is the perfect moment to stop and remember how strong God is! When we are at our strongest is the perfect moment to thank Him for everything He means to us.

BEING A WISE WOMAN IN A WILD WORLD
Robin Chaddock

What is wisdom in our topsy-turvy world? Professional success? Becoming wonderful wives and mothers? Life coach Robin Chaddock says, "It's not about priorities and getting everything all straightened out. It's about God loving you, and you living minute by minute in that eternal love." Robin helps you explore your unique personality and gifts to know God more intimately and put your passions and interests to work for Him. If you long to draw closer to God, Robin's fresh insights will really speak to your heart.

THE MOTHER-IN-LAW DANCE
Annie Chapman

A mother-in-law and daughter-in-law can become friends—even close friends. However this connectedness is a journey, and there will be bumps in the road. Offering real-life insights, thoughtful ideas, and biblical wisdom, Annie helps you deal with family traditions and activities, manage differences in handling money, cope with intrusive comments and actions, accept and reject child-rearing advice, and survive differences in faith.

A WOMAN'S SECRET TO A BALANCED LIFE
Lysa TerKeurst and Sharon Jaynes

Do you long to see God's purpose for your life fulfilled? Mining the principles of Proverbs 31, you'll learn seven vital ways to prioritize your life, including creating a loving environment for family and friends, faithfully overseeing time and money, and participating in community activities.

COMING OUT OF THE DARK
Mary Southerland

As a pastor's wife, Mary Southerland had it all...a successful career as a conference leader and women's ministry director, a husband who led a growing church, and two kids who were the joy of her life...until clinical depression brought her world crashing down. Mary's journey offers you hope if you struggle with depression, help if you have loved ones dealing with depression, and encouragement if you're in a dark time of life. If you dwell in the shadows, this book will guide you to the One who is light and the Giver of hope.

THE MOTHER LOAD
Mary M. Byers

Motherhood is an intense, 'round-the-clock job. To stay healthy, moms need friends, laughter, solitude, and an intimate relationship with the Lord. *The Mother Load* offers down-to-earth suggestions, spiritual truths, and real-life advice from moms to help you survive...and thrive!...in today's active family.

HARVEST HOUSE
PUBLISHERS